BEST OF INTENTIONS

BEST OF INTENTIONS

America's Campaign Against Strategic Weapons Proliferation

HENRY D. SOKOLSKI

Foreword by James Woolsey

Westport, Connecticut
London

Library of Congress Cataloging-in-Publication Data

Sokolski, Henry D.
  Best of intentions : America's campaign against strategic weapons proliferation /
Henry D. Sokolski ; Foreword by James Woolsey.
    p.   cm.
  Includes bibliographical references and index.
  ISBN 0–275–96752–2 (alk. paper)—ISBN 0–275–97289–5 (pbk. : alk. paper)
    1. Nuclear nonproliferation.   2. Nuclear nonproliferation—Government policy—
United States—History.   3. United States—Foreign relations—1989–   I. Title.
JZ5675.S66   2001
327.1'747—dc21   00–052845

British Library Cataloguing in Publication Data is available.

Library of Congress Catalog Card Number: 00–052845
ISBN: 0–275–96752–2
    0–275–97289–5 (pbk.)

First published in 2001

Praeger Publishers, 88 Post Road West, Westport, CT 06881
An imprint of Greenwood Publishing Group, Inc.
www.praeger.com

Printed in the United States of America

The paper used in this book complies with the
Permanent Paper Standard issued by the National
Information Standards Organization (Z39.48–1984).

10 9 8 7 6 5 4 3 2 1

To my father and Albert Wohlstetter,
two men who understood the importance
of clarity and persistence.

Contents

Photographic essay follows p. 86.

Foreword

Henry Sokolski has done us all a great service by parsing, briefly and succinctly, the tangled history of nonproliferation and by relating it to the problems we face today.

If you have trouble keeping the acronyms straight—or, more importantly, figuring out what the Baruch Plan, Atoms for Peace, the NPT, and the Nuclear Suppliers Group can teach us about Saddam threatening us someday with a nuclear-tipped missile—this fine volume is exactly what you need.

To give only one example of how Sokolski makes nonproliferation's past relevant and informative: he explains clearly how the Nuclear Nonproliferation Treaty came to be internally inconsistent, with its early articles focusing on preventing the spread of nuclear technology to nonnuclear countries and its later ones focusing on the need to limit the size of the two superpowers' arsenals. Today there is again tension between those who focus on blocking horizontal proliferation (i.e., preventing increasing numbers of nations from obtaining weapons of mass destruction and ballistic missiles and those who are much more concerned about the vertical variety (the size of the few nuclear powers' arsenals).

Sokolski leaves no doubt where he stands (and I would agree)—that horizontal proliferation is a problem in its own right and that we create serious difficulties in addressing it when we overemphasize the urgency for further U.S.-Russian arsenal reductions and concomitantly affirm mutual assured destruction and the targeting of civilians. (As one wag put this philosophy years ago, "Offense is defense. Defense is offense. Weapons that kill people are good. Weapons that kill weapons are bad. Keep that straight and everything else falls into place.") If we are instead able to persuade ourselves now, after the cold war, to move carefully and effectively to check the growing dangers of horizontal proliferation as we reduce existing arsenals, this excellent volume will be an important part of the reason.

James Woolsey

Preface: Why a Nonproliferation History?

When it comes to the spread of strategic weaponry, there is no lack of analysis. Detailed studies have examined why and how nuclear weapons states acquired their arsenals. Others have analyzed why states have reversed or stopped their strategic programs, while others still have considered whether or not such proliferation is stabilizing.[1]

Yet, in all this, perhaps the most critical policy question—how effective U.S. and international efforts have been in curbing such proliferation—has largely gone begging. That this question has gone unanswered is all the more striking in light of several clear nonproliferation successes. In the 1970s, Sweden terminated its nuclear weapons program. In the 1980s and very early 1990s, Taiwan, South Korea, Ukraine, Argentina, South Africa, and Brazil all foreswore or dismantled their nuclear weapons or long-range missile programs.

Were these events merely the result of domestic factors or were other nations' efforts against proliferation, led by the United States, somehow responsible? Focusing on the specific cases, this last question is difficult to answer. Certainly, U.S. alliance efforts under the North Atlantic Treaty Organization (NATO) repressed many European nations' nuclear ambitions (including Sweden's) but this was not NATO's primary purpose. Similarly, as a security guarantor, the United States has always had compelling reasons beyond nonproliferation for keeping South Korea from going ballistic or nuclear. Even where U.S.-led nonproliferation efforts clearly had a hand, as with South Africa's and Argentina's termination of their large rocket programs, it is difficult to know how much weight to give to these external efforts over domestic factors.

Matters are no less muddy in regard to known cases of nonproliferation failure. Here, too, the problem of determining causality looms large. From the 1950s on, the nuclear industry convinced the governments in the United States, Canada, France, and Germany to support the sale of nuclear technology to India, Pakistan, Israel, Iraq, Argentina, Iran, and Brazil. These sales, in turn, gave a major boost to the nuclear weapons programs in each of these developing nations. Did such corporate boosterism overtake the nonproliferation value of Dwight D. Eisenhower's Atoms for Peace Program or was the president's program prone to spread bomb-making capabilities with or without such lobbying? Similarly, after the fall of the shah in Tehran, the United States and its Western allies consciously downplayed Iraq's violation of its nonproliferation obligations. Given such willful inattention, does it make sense to use Iraq to judge the effectiveness of the Nuclear Nonproliferation Treaty (NPT) and the inspections it called for?

If one focuses on these specific cases, the precise cause of nonproliferation successes or failure is virtually impossible to divine. Yet, without some way to gauge the impact of U.S. and international nonproliferation initiatives, one cannot fully understand what was at play. Worse, one is resigned either to dismiss such nonproliferation efforts as being ineffective or to assume they were all beneficial even when they were not.

This suggests the alternative approach taken by this book. Rather than judge the effectiveness of key nonproliferation initiatives through the lens of specific cases, the book focuses first on the original logic and intent of the nonproliferation initiatives themselves. This approach has several advantages. First, it allows one to examine how sound each of these initiative's original rationale was and compare what each hoped to achieve with what each subsequently accomplished. Even before the Soviets vetoed the Baruch Plan, did this plan's key premises make sense? What about Atoms for Peace? Was it destined to spread nuclear weapons production technology no matter what the power or influence of the nuclear power industry was?

Second, by focusing on the original objectives of each nonproliferation initiative, this approach allows one to judge the relative merits of each effort without necessarily having to assess its impact on every known case of arms proliferation or restraint. Weren't the NPT's objectives as first articulated by the Irish Resolutions of 1958 more likely to encourage restraint than subsequent demands to have nuclear states share all forms of civilian nuclear technology? If so, wouldn't one's choice between these views bear directly on how the NPT might be implemented? Might this not explain how the treaty's enforcement has varied so radically (e.g., as between North Korea and Iraq)? Finally, by taking this approach to understanding nonproliferation, we can gain new insights as to what did and did not work and why—these insights, in turn, should help us learn how to do better in the future.

Certainly, it is in this spirit that this book has been written. It purposely has been kept brief to make it accessible to the informed lay reader as well as to students and teachers. Because the book's aim is to identify and weigh the premises of U.S. nonproliferation policies, it consciously avoids trying to describe every case of arms proliferation or restraint. Instead, the book is intended to introduce the reader to the most important nonproliferation initiatives and the rationales behind them.

It is divided into seven chapters. The first and last examine nonproliferation's past and future. The remaining chapters chronicle the key nonproliferation initiatives offered since 1945.

The book identifies five distinct nonproliferation undertakings—the Baruch Plan, the Atoms for Peace Program, the Nuclear Nonproliferation Treaty (NPT), proliferation technology control regimes, and counterproliferation. Although the announcement of each of these efforts followed the other chronologically, most either overlapped or built on one another. The NPT, for example, clearly built on the safeguards system fostered by the Atoms for Peace Program. Yet, each initiative is substantively distinct from the other regarding the strategic threat that each assumed needed to be mitigated most. How sound these views were, in turn, largely determined the strengths and weaknesses of each initiative. To the extent each characterized the strategic threat properly, they produced nonproliferation measures that were sound. To the extent they did not, they encouraged measures that were impractical or that actually compounded the proliferation threats they were supposed to reduce.

NOTE

1. For a review of contemporary proliferation-related scholarship, see Tanya Ogilvie-White, "Is There a Theory of Nuclear Proliferation? An Analysis of the Contemporary Debate," *The Nonproliferation Review* (Fall 1996): 43–60; Zachary S. Davis and Benjamin Frankel, eds., *The Proliferation Puzzle: Why Nuclear Weapons Spread and What Results* (London: Frank Cass, 1993); and Peter R. Lavoy, "Nuclear Myths and the Causes of Nuclear Proliferation," *Security Studies* (Spring/Summer 1993): 199ff.

Acknowledgments

In giving credit for truly long projects, there is a temptation to start at creation. I have rarely discussed this book with my mother, but, ultimately she is at fault for nearly everything I have done. I have already dedicated the book to my father. As for my brother and sister, they ought not to be blamed in any respect.

This leaves most of my professional friends and the institutions that have lent direct support to this project. First among these is the Earhart Foundation, whose early encouragement and support first engaged me in this project. Their desire was for a short book designed to teach and provoke thought. They have been extremely patient. Also, among the ranks of early supporters, is the United States Institute of Peace, which has generously lent support both to this project and to the educational activities of my nonprofit educational organization, the Nonproliferation Policy Education Center. During this project's first year, the National Institute for Public Policy, and its director Keith Payne, also graciously hosted me as a visiting fellow. To all of these institutions, I extend heartfelt thanks.

Although critical, none of these foundations' assistance would have been sufficient were it not for the sustaining grants of the Smith Richardson Foundation and the William H. Donner Foundation. These foundations not only helped create and sustain the nonprofit educational center I now direct, but lent me moral support through the guidance of their senior program managers. To Marin Stremcki, Jim Capua, and William Alpert, I owe a personal debt of gratitude which I will never be able to repay.

The impetus for this book came from the instruction of Albert Wohlstetter at the University of Chicago. He and Roberta Wohlstetter joined the advisory board of my center in 1994. Whatever is sound in this volume is their doing and that of their associates, Henry S. Rowen and Andrew Marshall, for whom I had the honor of having worked in the Department of Defense. Victor Gilinsky, who also serves on my center's advisory board, has also guided my thinking in ways more powerful than he knows.

Others have had the unfortunate burden of having to struggle with this volume's draft text. Principal among these is Ms. Marianne Oliva, my center's research coordinator. Marianne not only prepared the bibliography and index but endured endless hours of copyediting and my own ramblings as to what I was trying to convey. Despite having clear cause, she never complained. I would also like to thank Tom Riisager, the center's Russian research fellow. To the extent that the volume's notes are correct, it is at least as much his doing as mine. Finally, I want to thank my copyeditor, Carol Blumentritt, and Jim Dunton, editorial consultant to the publisher, whose courtesy and persistent reminders actually got me to complete the book.

Finally, a number of close friends were kind enough to review the manuscript. Those who kept my confidence during the book's roughest drafts, but who were also always frank, included Steve Cambone, Seth Carus, Joe Cirincione, Mark Clark, Alberto Coll, Richard Cupitt, Zachary Davis, Robin Dorff, Peter Feaver, Victor Gilinsky, Dan Goure, Allen Grebb, Richard Haass, Peter Hays, Fred Ikle, William Kristol, Mark Lagon, Robert Lawrence, Mary Lovegrove, Tom Mahnken, Gordon Oehler, Keith Payne, George Perkovich, Robert Pfaltzgraff, Joe Pilat, George Quester, Peter Rodman, Mitchell Reiss, Brad Roberts, Henry Rowen, Amy Sands, Gary Schmitt, Richard Starr, Paul Viotti, Frank von Hippel, Len Weiss, Bill Williamson, Randy Willoughby, and James Woolsey. Each, in many respects, could have written a better book. Certainly, whatever errors they did not catch are mine alone.

1

The First Half Century

Among the military threats facing the world's nations, few are of greater significance than the spread of strategic weapons. Indeed, preventing such proliferation has been a concern since the advent of nuclear energy. Then, as today, the worry has been that the spread of just a few strategic weapons would guarantee total victory to any aggressor against even the strongest of nations. Since then, biological and chemical weapons as well as long-range cruise and ballistic missiles have been added to the list. As with nuclear weapons, the use of even a few of these systems could produce war-winning or victory-denying (i.e., strategic) results against adversaries great or small. Nor are there any truly effective military countermeasures against these systems. One can limit the damage they might inflict by hiding in deep bunkers or donning awkward protective gear, but countermeasures of the sort that our military employs to neutralize enemy air defense radars with jammers and the like are not yet available. Proliferation, then, relates to all the issues concerning the spread of such high-leverage strategic weaponry.

What nonproliferation is, on the other hand, is not nearly as clear. Nonproliferation, after all, is measured in terms of the events it prevents. But, how does one pinpoint the cause of a nonevent? Does it matter that there are different approaches to prompting such restraint? Are all attempts at nonproliferation equally valid, or are some self-defeating and others truly effective? What might explain their success or failure?

These are the questions that animate this book. It is divided into seven sections. The first and last examine nonproliferation's past and future.

The remaining chapters chronicle the key nonproliferation initiatives offered since 1945. As already explained in the book's preface, not every proliferation event is detailed. Instead, the book is intended to introduce the reader to the most important nonproliferation initiatives and the rationales behind them.

The book identifies five distinct nonproliferation undertakings—the Baruch Plan, the Atoms for Peace Program, the Nuclear Nonproliferation Treaty (NPT), proliferation technology control regimes, and counterproliferation. Although the announcement of each of these efforts followed the other chronologically, most either overlapped or built on one another. The NPT, for example, clearly built on the safeguards system fostered by the Atoms for Peace Program. Yet, each initiative is substantively distinct from the other regarding the strategic threat that each assumed needed to be mitigated most. How sound these views were, in turn, largely determined the strengths and weaknesses of each initiative. To the extent each characterized the strategic threat properly, they produced nonproliferation measures that were sound. To the extent they did not, they encouraged measures that were impractical or that actually compounded the proliferation threats they were supposed to reduce.

DISARMING PROLIFERATION: BARUCH, ATOMS FOR PEACE, AND THE NPT

As already noted, what strategic dangers needed to be avoided meant something different to each nonproliferation initiative. In the case of the Baruch Plan, which the United States offered to the United Nations (UN) in 1946, though, the plan's virtues and vices ultimately were a function of its assumptions concerning the inability to deflect offensive nuclear wars. As is detailed in chapter 2, the Baruch Plan assumed that the spread of nuclear weapons would automatically prompt undeterrable atomic wars for which there could be no defense. As such, the plan was extremely strict in how it proposed to control nuclear activities and materials.

Anything critical to bomb making was branded as being dangerous and placed under the control of an international atomic energy authority. Only nuclear activities and materials that could not readily be diverted to military purposes were considered to be safe enough for nations to own or conduct and, then, only under rigorous international inspections. Much of this scheme, particularly the attempt to distinguish between safe and dangerous nuclear activities and materials, had merit. Yet, the plan's exaggerated fears of undeterrable offensive nuclear wars at once made it clearly desirable for the United States to retain possession of nuclear weapons as long as possible and, thus, encouraged the Soviets to reject the plan. Certainly, if nuclear weapons ensured victory for the aggressor, the Soviets were unlikely to agree to renounce acquisition so long as the United States retained a nuclear monopoly.

The strategic assumptions prevalent during the Eisenhower administration were no less significant in determining the efficacy of its nonproliferation effort, the Atoms for Peace Program. As explained in chapter 3, what President Eisenhower proposed was directly shaped by what U.S. strategic planners feared the most: Soviet acquisition of enough nuclear weapons to destroy (or "knock out") America's military-industrial mobilization base (i.e., 100 of America's largest cities).

To put off the day Moscow might acquire such a stockpile, Eisenhower suggested that Russia and the United States make joint contributions of nuclear weapons fissile material (i.e., plutonium and highly enriched uranium) to an international atomic energy agency. This agency, the International Atomic Energy Agency (IAEA), was supposed to accept fissile material from the world's nuclear states to fuel peaceful nuclear power projects worldwide. The more nuclear power grew, the more the Russians would have to contribute and the more remote would be Moscow's ability to destroy the United States.

The IAEA was also supposed to safeguard the nuclear projects it sponsored to ensure no nation ever diverted enough nuclear material to knock out any other state. Eisenhower also hoped that the IAEA might supervise a military fissile production cut-off treaty that he proposed in 1956 (as "the logical conclusion and follow-through of the Atoms for Peace Plan"). If it fulfilled this broader role, many hoped the IAEA might provide the kind of nuclear control the Baruch Plan never achieved.

Unfortunately, the program's authors misunderstood the strategic threat they faced. In fact, U.S. Air Force-sponsored analyses determined in the early 1950s that the Soviets might prevail in war without targeting any of America's key cities. All the Soviets required was to attack America's relatively vulnerable strategic air bases—a target set that needed scores of bombs, not hundreds or thousands as U.S. policy planners assumed. As for smaller nations, they could conceivably ignite a nuclear war between the United States and Russia with only a single bomb (whether fired intentionally or by accident). Instead of being vulnerable to a massive nuclear "knockout blow" stockpile of hundreds or thousands of weapons, the security of the United States and other nations could be jeopardized with one or a relatively small force.

This strategic miscalculation put much of the Atoms for Peace Program at odds with its nonproliferation intent. For one thing, the safeguards the program recommended and that the states negotiating the IAEA ultimately adopted were egregiously loose. They hardly were designed to detect the diversion of a weapon's worth of nuclear material or do so early enough to prevent its military diversion. The goal instead was merely to sound an alarm *after* massive military diversions of fissile (a hundred weapons' worth or more) threatened to give a nation a "knock-out blow capability" against the United States. Then, there was the program's enthusiasm for sharing civilian nuclear technology—know-how, materials, and hardware that were of direct use for making bombs. Coupled together, these two attributes resulted in the Atoms for Peace program fueling more proliferation than it curbed.

The Nuclear Nonproliferation Treaty was negotiated, in part, to correct this. Proposed to the UN by Irish Foreign Minister Fredrick Aiken in 1958, the NPT originally was focused against the threat that the addition of even one nuclear weapons state with only one weapon might pose to international security.

As detailed in chapter 4, the first concern with such "horizontal" proliferation (i.e., the quantitative increase in the number of nations possessing strategic weapons) was the instability it would foster. How might the existing nuclear powers respond to a nuclear attack against them launched either accidentally or intentionally by one of these new nuclear states? Could any superpower know for sure that such attacks were not, in fact, fired or ordered by one of their declared foes? If not, what would keep them from massively (and mistakenly) counterattacking one another? The second concern had to do with disarmament. It was challenging enough to get Britain, the United States, and Russia to agree to limit their nuclear arms. What would happen to the prospects for arms control if the number of nations that would have to agree to such limits doubled or quadrupled?

These strategic challenges, arms experts argued, threatened the security of both the superpowers and the nonweapons states alike. Against these dangers, the Irish proposed a simple but tough bargain. The nuclear states would agree not to spread nuclear weapons to nonweapons states and the world's nonweapons states would, in turn, foreswear developing such weapons and open their civilian nuclear programs to international inspections. This original NPT bargain is reflected in the treaty's first three articles.

Unfortunately, two things prevented early agreement to this deal. First, Russia and the United States initially could not agree to any non-proliferation treaty until they determined how they might deploy their own weapons on foreign soil. Second, by the time agreement on the NATO and Warsaw Pact deployments was reached in the mid-1960s, most NPT negotiators no longer viewed the strategic threat as they had in 1958. Instead of horizontal proliferation, most viewed the primary threat to international security to be vertical proliferation—that is, the quantitative and qualitative build-up of the superpowers' strategic arsenals.

Now, the greatest threat of nuclear war seemed to be the superpowers' amassing ever quicker reaction weapons (aimed at the other side's weapons and defenses) under the loosening command of a growing number of military officers. Such arms competitions and the risks of accidental war and unauthorized firings they might engender was the central concern of a new strategic theory called finite deterrence. According to this school of thought, making nuclear weapons more accurate, using them against military targets or trying to defend against their delivery systems only heightened the arms race and, thus, made accidental and intentional wars more likely. Finite deterrence proponents condemned such competitions and instead believed that nations could mutually deter one another by merely acquiring a relative few crude nuclear weapons to target their adversaries' largest cities.

Operating under these new strategic assumptions, NPT negotiators insisted that the nuclear weapons states agree to work to end their nuclear arms competitions and eventually to disarm. In exchange, the nonweapons states agreed not to exercise their right to acquire finite nuclear deterrent stockpiles of their own unless the superpowers failed to reduce their own arsenals or a neighbor acquired a nuclear arsenal.

An additional condition for nonweapons states adhering to this new NPT bargain was that the nuclear weapons states offer them the "fullest possible exchange" of "peaceful" nuclear technology. The thinking here was that nonweapons states who foreswore acquiring nuclear weapons should not be deprived of the civilian benefits of nuclear energy that the nuclear weapons states had already mastered.

All of this rationale was internally consistent. However, it raised several nonproliferation difficulties. Because the nonweapons states claimed that they were only interested in acquiring "peaceful" forms of nuclear energy, they were resistant to anything but the least intrusive forms of international inspections. Indeed, intrusive inspections, they insisted, were unnecessary: The key protection against proliferation was to be found in the willingness of nonweapons states to sign the NPT and, thus, formally to forego their right to acquire nuclear weapons. Yet, the technology needed to make nuclear power enabled its possessors to make weapons-usable uranium and plutonium and, thus, could bring nations to within days or weeks of acquiring a nuclear arsenal of their own.

Even more disturbing, was that the new NPT articles that reflected finite deterrence thinking—Articles IV, VI, and X—implicitly endorsed nonweapons states acquiring sensitive nuclear technology and for them to break out of the treaty if "extraordinary events" related to the treaty "jeopardized" their "supreme interests." Certainly, total nuclear disarmament was the preferred path. But if nonweapons states felt threatened by their neighbors or believed that the superpowers were not sufficiently forthcoming on either arms reductions or nuclear cooperation, then using the most sensitive "peaceful" nuclear technology to acquire a crude finite deterrent might make sense.

FIGHTING A RISING TIDE: PROLIFERATION CONTROL REGIMES AND COUNTERPROLIFERATION

None of these subtleties were lost on the United States or other nuclear supplier states. Indeed, shortly after the ink was dry on the NPT, officials from these states met secretly to determine how to work outside of the NPT to restrict the transfer of sensitive nuclear technology to the world's trouble spots. This Nuclear Suppliers Group (NSG), established in 1974, then became a model for restricting sensitive missile, chemical, and biological agent materials and technology under the Missile Technology Control Regime (MTCR) and the Australia Group (AG).

As explained in chapter 5, the underlying strategic worry of these control efforts was that with proliferation to such hot spots as the Middle East and South West Asia, regional wars were likely to go ballistic or nuclear. Such conflagrations, in turn, would inevitably draw in the United States and the Soviet Union, since both were engaged in a much larger struggle to dominate world events. Although regional concerns prompted these proliferation control regimes' creation, their abiding strategic context, as such, was the cold war.

When the Soviet Union collapsed in 1990, political support for these technology control regimes naturally declined, and a new rationale for their continued promotion was necessary. A key aspect of these regimes' unpopularity was their discriminatory tone. To remedy this, the United States offered to include proliferators, such as Russia and China, in the MTCR and the AG in exchange for their promises to sign other arms control agreements such as the NPT, the Chemical Weapons Convention (CWC), and the Comprehensive Test Ban Treaty (CTBT). Once these new states were included in these control regimes, they were rewarded with freer access to the strategic technology that these control efforts previously kept from them.

This effort to include other strategic weapons supplier nations, including known proliferators, succeeded in expanding the MTCR, NSG, and the AG. It also undermined their enforcement. In fact, U.S. nonproliferation sanctions explicitly exempted members of these control regimes from most penalties. In addition, these new members were less interested in tightening the regimes' controls than in gaining access to the technology they covered. To the extent that supplier state businesses supported dropping as many trade controls as possible, the push for decontrol became at least as strong as the residual interest in maintaining or expanding such strategic technology trade restrictions.

Realism and the war against an Iraq armed with chemical and biological weapons and missiles gave rise to the U.S. Department of Defense's Counterproliferation Initiative. As explained in chapter 6, the original idea behind this initiative was that if nonproliferation failed, the Defense

Department would have to develop military means to neutralize proliferation threats. Defense officials assumed this was possible. The question was how.

Initially, officials focused on pre-emptive strikes against nascent nuclear, chemical, biological, and missile programs such as the one that the Israelis staged against Iraq's nuclear program in 1981. This approach, however, flew in the face of an American tradition opposed to Pearl Harbor-like strikes. It also underestimated the difficulties of targeting such programs. After objections were raised over taking such an approach, the initiative reverted to a more modest set of objectives—deterring strategic weapons strikes against United States and allied forces and limiting damage if such weapons were used.

Even this more humble set of objectives, though, raised a number of problems. How, for example, could the United States deter chemical and biological weapons use with threats of nuclear retaliation without encouraging nations to acquire nuclear weapons as well? Also, in developing ways to operate and prevail against other nations' uses of chemical, biological, or nuclear munitions, was the United States suggesting that it was giving up on the promotion of nonproliferation and would tolerate the use of such weapons?

Lacking the answers to these questions, counterproliferation supporters largely returned to emphasizing damage limitation—passive defenses against chemical, biological, and conventional missile attacks and active missile defenses and counterattacks. The consequence of this emphasis was the bureaucratic downgrading of the initiative within the Pentagon.

Again, this initiative's shortcomings are related to its strategic premises. Initially, its attraction to pre-emption simply ignored American culture. Also, the initiative presumed that there was a military means to neutralize proliferation problems. In fact, this is quite difficult, if not impossible, to achieve. Weapons that are of proliferation concern, after all, are precisely those systems against which we lack effective military countermeasures and whose use even in relatively small numbers could produce war-winning or victory-denying results. To presume that there is some military-technical solution to proliferation, therefore, is to misunderstand the threat it presents.

This review of nonproliferation efforts, and their strategic presumptions are summarized in Table 1.

LESSONS FOR THE NEXT NONPROLIFERATION CAMPAIGN

As is detailed in the concluding chapter, this nonproliferation history teaches at least three things. First, several of these nonproliferation ini-

Table 1
Nonproliferation Initiatives and Their Strategic Premises

Initiative	Strategic Premise	Control Effort
Baruch UN Proposal (1946)	Aggressor always wins. There's no defense or effective means of deterrence.	International ownership of all dangerous nuclear activities; nuclear weapons disarmament.
Atoms for Peace Program, creation of the IAEA (1953)	Knockout blow against 100 U.S. military industrial cities would cripple the nation.	Draw foreign nuclear stockpiles below knockout blow levels by joint contributions of fissile to an IAEA that would promote civilian nuclear projects and guard against large diversions.
Irish Resolutions, early NPT treaty negotiations (1958)	Catalytic and accidental nuclear wars between the Superpowers could be prompted by horizontal proliferation.	Get weapons states not to share nuclear weapons or means to make them; get nonweapons states not to acquire and to agree to inspections to ensure this.

Table 1 (*Continued*)

Initiative	Strategic Premise	Control Effort
NPT, its final negotiation (1968)	Superpower arms racing beyond finite deterrence requirements will lead to international instability, wars that small nations will want to hedge against by getting their own strategic weapons.	Get weapons states to disarm and to share civil nuclear technology and nonweapons states to forgo their "right" to strategic arms.
NSG, MTCR, AG (1974, 1985, 1987)	Regional catalytic and accidental wars using missiles armed with weapons capable of mass destruction will draw in cold war superpowers.	Deny nonweapons states access to strategic weapons technology by creating discriminatory suppliers clubs.
Counterproliferation (1993)	Regional powers using weapons capable of mass destruction and long-range missiles could defeat U.S. or allied forces.	Develop military means to neutralize nuclear, biological and chemical weapons and long-range missiles and to limit the damage they might inflict.

tiatives and their strategic assumptions are still in play. Second, the shortcomings and strengths of each initiative suggest a series of possible correctives for the future. Finally, basing nonproliferation initiatives primarily on assessments of how future strategic wars might emerge is risky.

Certainly, to an extent not properly appreciated, current U.S. nonproliferation efforts still reflect past nonproliferation assumptions. The finite deterrence thinking that animated the NPT's final negotiations, for example, is very much in evidence in the case of the U.S. 1994 nuclear deal with North Korea. U.S. nonproliferation policy toward Iran and Iraq, on the other hand, is much more reflective of the toughness of the Baruch Plan. One could generate more examples. The broader point, however, is that understanding the rationales behind past nonproliferation initiatives gives us a deeper understanding of the strengths and weaknesses of their policy analogs today.

This, then, brings us to the second point, which is that thinking through the key strengths and shortcomings of past nonproliferation initiatives offers something of a guide to what the next campaign against proliferation should aspire to and avoid. The Baruch Plan's rigorous standards for what effective safeguards require and its distinction between safe and dangerous nuclear activities certainly recommend themselves now as the nuclear states tackle the nettlesome issue of fissile material controls. In contrast, the casual approach the Atoms for Peace Program took to safeguards suggests what to avoid. What the program rightly struggled with is the connection between reducing existing weapons arsenals and curbing their further spread. Unfortunately, it got the connection wrong with disastrous results.

This last point could be applied just as well to the finite deterrence arguments made to promote the NPT. In fact, this theory—that nations can secure stability and security with a few crude nuclear weapons targeted against other nations' cities so long as no state tries to develop defenses against such attacks—actually tends to make the acquisition of a crude strategic force *more* attractive. On the other hand, the arguments made by the Irish, who launched the NPT's negotiation, still seem sensible and have the reverse effect.

What might we learn from America's experience with proliferation technology controls and sanctions? Here, what stands out is the extent to which efforts to expand the MTCR, AG, and NSG by giving proliferators incentives to join may have weakened these efforts. Indeed, given the amount of trade now done in strategic technology with proliferating Indian, Chinese, and Russian enterprises, the United States would do well today merely to end direct U.S. subsidies and technological support to such entities.

Finally, the shortcomings of the Counterproliferation Initiative suggest the futility of relying on military technical fixes. As is noted in the concluding chapter, perhaps the most important historical nonproliferation lesson of all is to avoid basing one's efforts so much on military analyses or assumptions. Indeed, each key initiative the United States has adopted against proliferation has fallen short largely because, to varying degrees, each has failed to fully understand the character of the strategic threat it was designed to address.

Instead of basing the next campaign solely on some theory or insight concerning emerging strategic military developments, it would make more sense to focus on trends that are more certain. Luckily, several political, economic, and social trends have emerged in the last three decades that are much easier to divine and that are likely to be far more significant in determining our proliferation fate. These nonmilitary trends promise growth in real wealth, liberal democratization, and demilitarization for an increasing number of nations.

Indeed, properly marshaled, these progressive trends could obviate current concerns about strategic weapons proliferation. However, even the most optimistic of analysts recognize that there are clear exceptions to such liberalization. Several Arab Islamic nations (even when the oil-rich ones are excluded) have gotten richer, more educated, and healthier *without* becoming more democratic. There also are serious debates among the experts over the middle- and long-term political futures of China and Russia. These exceptions are hardly trivial: From a proliferation standpoint, they include the most serious actors.

Hence, if one is serious about combating proliferation without waging actual wars, new strategies will have to be devised that leverage our economic, political, and technical strengths against the enduring weaknesses of the most worrisome proliferators. Certainly, this much is clear: The next campaign against proliferation, if it is to succeed, cannot treat all nations alike. It must have a much clearer stake in promoting liberal democracy over those regimes that are hostile to such self-rule.

2
The Baruch Plan

More than any other nonproliferation or arms control proposal, the Baruch Plan was influenced by the creators of nuclear weapons. As one historian noted, from 1945 to 1947 these scientists began to "act into history as they once acted into nature."[1]

The most important and earliest vehicles for such influence were three nuclear energy studies prepared for the U.S. government. The first, the Jeffries Report (sometimes referred to as the Prospectus on Nucleonics), was written for Arthur Compton, director of the Manhattan Project's plutonium production efforts. It suggested what lay ahead in developing nuclear energy and was passed on to General Leslie Groves, the commanding officer of the Manhattan Project. The second study, the Franck Report, was also prepared under Compton and was sent to U.S. Secretary of War Henry Stimson. Its aim was to explore how the development of atomic energy might be controlled after the war. The third report was requested by Under Secretary of State Dean Acheson. It was written in 1946 by several of the Manhattan Project's top managers to help devise a specific plan of international control for atomic energy. Backed by the American scientists' movement and the U.S. Congress, this study, known as the Acheson-Lilienthal Report, served as the basis of U.S. UN representative Bernard Baruch's proposal before the United Nations Atomic Energy Commission to create an international atomic energy control authority.[2]

THE AGGRESSOR WILL ALWAYS WIN

Although varied in their specific charters, all three of these studies were unified in their view of the threat nuclear weapons posed. First, they all agreed that nuclear weapons gave an unqualified advantage to the aggressor. As the Jeffries Report explained:

Nuclear power, beyond any older means of warfare, holds out to the aggressor the temptation of being able to make a successful sudden stroke, even a vastly more powerful and well-prepared nation. . . . A nation given the opportunity to start aggression by a sudden use of nuclear destruction devices, will be able to unleash a blitzkrieg infinitely more terrifying than that of 1939–40. A sudden blow of this kind might literally wipe out even the largest nation, or at least all of its production centers, and decide the issue on the first day of the war. The weight of the weapons of destruction required to deliver this blow will be infinitesimal compared to that used up in a present day heavy bombing raid.[3]

Thus, the spread of nuclear energy presented the U.S. with an increasingly intolerable threat:

Since the area of the earth does not increase, the advantage of the attacker constantly increases with increasing technical development. If two people are in a room of 100 by 100 feet and have no weapons except their bare fists, the attacker has only a slight advantage over his opponent. But if each of them has a machine gun in his hands the attacker is sure to be victorious. With the production of nuclear bombs, however, the world situation approaches that of two men with machine guns in a 100 by 100 foot room.[4]

The Franck Report, written by some of the same authors as the Jeffries Report, reiterated that nuclear weapons advantaged offensive action and argued against the notion that the United States could stay ahead in a nuclear competition:

A quantitative advantage in reserves of bottled destructive power will not make us safe from sudden attack. Just because a potential enemy will be afraid of being "outnumbered and outgunned," the temptation for him may be overwhelming to attempt a sudden unprovoked blow, particularly if he should suspect us of harboring aggressive intentions against his security or his sphere of influence. In no other type of warfare does the advantage lie so heavily with the aggressor.[5]

Finally, both the Acheson-Lilienthal Report and the Baruch Plan adopted the notion that nuclear weapons favored the aggressor by arguing that the spread of nuclear weapons would inevitably lead to war. Thus, the atomic bomb was "an instrument of war so terrible that its uncontrolled development would not only intensify the ferocity of warfare, but might directly contribute to the outbreak of war" and force "a choice between the quick and the dead."[6]

A second key premise reflected in these studies (and also in a joint allied declaration concerning the international control of nuclear energy) was that "there can be no adequate military defense."[7] Any threats of retaliation, no matter how frightening, could not prevent the devastation of an aggressor's initial strike. Air defenses could never be effective enough, and the dispersal of U.S. cities and industrial plants was, at best, an expensive stopgap measure.[8]

SAFEGUARDS AND TIMELY WARNING

What, then, was to be done? Nothing less than the creation of an international authority to control and take ownership of the means of atomic production. Indeed, given the decisive offensive character of nuclear weapons, mere international inspections of national nuclear activities would only make matters worse. As the Acheson-Lilienthal report explained:

Take the case of a controlled reactor, a power pile, producing plutonium. Assume an international agreement barring use of the plutonium in a bomb, but permitting use of the pile for heat or power. No system of inspection, we have concluded, could afford any reasonable security against the diversion of such materials to the purpose of war. If nations may engage in this dangerous field, and only national good faith and international policing stand in the way, *the very existence of the prohibition* [italics added] against the use of such piles to produce fissionable material suitable for bombs would tend to stimulate and encourage surreptitious evasions.[9]

As long as nuclear weapons gave such a clear offensive advantage to their possessors, inspections and prohibitions against their possible production from civilian nuclear facilities would only encourage countries to cheat. The only way around this problem was to prohibit nations from owning *anything* that might help them make a bomb and—as the Baruch Plan emphasized—to ensure that the penalties for violating the prohibitions were "swift and condign."

Under the Acheson-Lilienthal Report and the Baruch Plan, then, all potentially dangerous nuclear activities, including fissionable material production, atomic explosives research, mining, and the refining of uranium and thorium, were to be owned and conducted by the proposed International Atomic Energy Authority alone. The idea was to control nuclear activities and materials so that any nuclear diversions would be noticed well before any nuclear explosive could be built. The international authority's safeguards system, had to give "unambiguous and reliable danger signals if a nation takes steps that do or may indicate the beginning of atomic warfare. Those danger signals must flash early enough to leave time adequate to permit other nations, alone or in concert, to take appropriate action."[10] This notion that the validity of nuclear safeguards depends on their ability to provide "timely warning" of diversions is still central to contemporary controversies surrounding safeguards.[11] Beyond this, the Acheson-Lilienthal Report and the Baruch Plan were quite prescient about the military potential of most civil nuclear activities. Indeed, both rightly emphasized that most nuclear activities and materials were so close to bomb making that no safeguard procedures could ever provide timely warning of their possible military diversion. Thus, they concluded that the atomic energy authority had to own, manage, and oversee all aspects of the nuclear fuel cycle if nations were to be kept from the edge of nuclear war.

As for sanctions, the Baruch Plan went even further than the Acheson-Lilienthal Report. The Acheson-Lilienthal Report noted that it would take a nation at least a year to make nuclear weapons and relied on diplomacy and the threat of war to deter and punish nations that violated the rules established by the proposed International Atomic Energy Authority. This seemed awkward and inadequate to Mr. Baruch. As he explained, even after the atomic energy authority was established, nations could make weapons:

As matters now stand, several years may be necessary for another country to produce a bomb, *de novo*. However, once the basic information is generally known, and the Authority has established production plants for peaceful purposes in several countries, an illegal seizure of such a plant might permit a malevolent nation to produce a bomb in 12 months, and if preceded by secret preparation and necessary facilities perhaps even in a much shorter time.[12]

For this reason, Baruch believed that the atomic energy authority had to have a variety of effective powers to punish nations that seized authority-owned or licensed plants or property or that tried to develop dangerous nuclear materials or facilities of their own.

Effective powers to inflict "condign punishment," though, required that an exception be made to the UN Charter and its condition that penalization of UN members come only with the concurrence of all five great powers—the Soviet Union, the United States, the United Kingdom, China, and France. Indeed, given what Baruch saw as the decisively offensive character of the bomb, maintaining this aspect of the UN Charter in the case of nuclear violations was a prescription for trouble. As he explained:

There must be no veto to protect those who violate their solemn agreements not to develop or to use atomic energy for destructive purposes. The bomb does not wait upon debate. To delay may be to die. The time between violation and pre-ventive action or punishment would be all too short for extended discussion as to the course to be followed.[13]

Why would the Soviet Union or any other nation agree to such a strict control regime? The authors of the Acheson-Lilienthal Report believed that nations had to be made to understand that submitting to the atomic energy authority was necessary to avoid the horrific dangers that nuclear armament would otherwise present. They understood, however, that making such a negative appeal was unlikely to carry the day and that the plan also had to appeal to "man's almost universal striving to im-prove his standard of living and his control of nature." Therefore, they insisted that the authority also had to promote the sharing of nuclear energy's "peaceful" benefits, particularly power reactor technology, which they claimed to be so "vital" to nations' economic development that even the Soviet Union would be drawn to the plan.[14]

DENATURING: AN UNHELPFUL ATTEMPT TO PROMOTE NUCLEAR POWER

The key danger with sharing nuclear power, however, was that power reactors produced not just electric power, but plutonium that might be used to make nuclear weapons. The report's authors tried to solve this difficulty by denying that the plutonium generated in power reactors could be used to make bombs. Here, they insisted that the plutonium that power reactors produced had so little of the plutonium isotopes optimal for weapons construction (i.e., plutonium 239 and 241) that the material could be considered "denatured," that is, unusable for military purposes.

Thus, the report distinguished between "safe" and "dangerous" reac-tors. Safe reactors included nuclear piles optimized for power production (but not for production of plutonium 239 and 241) and very small re-search reactors that could not produce a weapon's worth of plutonium, even over a period of several years. Both of these safe reactor types would be fueled with either low enrichment uranium (which, unlike highly enriched uranium, lacked sufficient fissile content, that is, high enough concentrations of U235, to make uranium weapons) or a mix of depleted uranium (U238) and denatured plutonium.

In contrast to these safe types were dangerous reactors, such as breeder and military production reactors. These were dangerous on several counts. First, they were optimized for plutonium production. Second, they could be fueled with weapons-usable fissile materials (for example, separated plutonium, thorium, and enriched uranium, which could be directly used to make bombs). Third, they could produce large quantities of the most readily weaponizable kinds of fuel: plutonium 239 and 241.

Clearly the world would be better off if safe reactors alone could supply its demand for nuclear electricity. The report's authors, however, did
not think this was possible. Why? In the mid and late 1940s, nuclear
scientists incorrectly assumed that U235 was extremely scarce. As such,
the report's authors concluded that the only way nuclear power could
be made viable was if plutonium-based fuels were utilized. These fuels
would be produced principally in "dangerous" breeder reactors capable
of making large quantities of plutonium from natural and depleted uranium. Under this scheme, then, the authority would build roughly as
many dangerous breeder plutonium-fuel producing reactors as safe
power systems configured to burn the plutonium that these breeders
produced.[15]

Technically, this scheme had problems. Plutonium, even if generated
in safe power reactors, could be used to make deliverable kiloton-yield
weapons. Such reactor-grade plutonium might not be "optimal" for this
purpose, but it was good enough and had to be considered dangerous.
Curiously, the report's authors were aware of this possibility. J. Robert
Oppenheimer, the Manhattan Project's chief scientist and advocate of
international atomic controls, pushed the plutonium denaturing argument in the report's first draft. In part, he may have hoped that the
possibility of using reactor-grade plutonium in bombs would not be easily realized. Clearly, he wanted to promote international controls and the
widespread use of nuclear power, which might give nations, such as the
Soviet Union, the incentive they needed to submit to such controls.

Yet, after examining the report, General Groves and the Manhattan
Project's other top scientists were concerned that Oppenheimer had gone
too far. They persuaded Oppenheimer to join them in qualifying the
value of denaturing in a memorandum to the Department of State that
was subsequently attached to the final report. Unfortunately, this qual-
ification was garbled. On the one hand, the memo lent qualified support
for denaturing:

For the various atomic explosives the denaturant has a different effect on the
explosive properties of the materials. In some cases denaturing will not completely preclude making atomic weapons but will reduce their effectiveness by
a large factor. The effect of the denaturant is also different in the peaceful application of the materials. . . . But it seems to us most probable that within the
framework of the proposals advanced in the State Department Report denaturing
will play a helpful part.[16]

The memorandum noted that in the case of uranium, denaturing (the
blending of fissile U235 with nonfissile U238) would prevent the use of
uranium in bombs but only so long as nations did not construct enrichment plants (which would take no more than one to three years to build).
With regard to plutonium, the memorandum noted, "In some cases de-

naturing will not completely preclude making atomic weapons, but will reduce their effectiveness by a large factor."[17]

Yet, in the end, the memorandum concluded that "the Report does not contend nor is it, in fact, true that a system of control based solely on denaturing could provide adequate safety." Indeed, it emphasized that "denaturing, though valuable in adding to the flexibility of a system of controls, cannot of itself eliminate the dangers of atomic warfare."[18]

Unfortunately, these warnings about the pitfalls of relying on denaturing went unnoted in the text of the report and continue to be misunderstood even today.[19] Yet, for all of their importance, they did not undermine the report's key finding that safe nuclear activities and materials needed to be distinguished from dangerous ones and that the latter needed to be removed from national control. Dangerous plutonium production reactors, fuel fabrication and reprocessing plants, uranium mines, enrichment plants, and nuclear weapons fuels were to be owned solely by the international authority. As an additional security measure, the report recommended that dangerous nuclear plants be spread geographically so that illicit seizure of any one plant by one nation could be neutralized or countered by other nations' seizure of plants located on their territory. This, the report's authors argued, would help further deter violations and help hedge against any nation's surprise acquisition of nuclear weapons.[20]

REJECTION

The Soviets, however, were not persuaded. Indeed, the presumed, unqualified offensive value of nuclear weapons (the worry at the core of the Acheson-Lilienthal Report and the Baruch Plan) and America's nuclear weapons monopoly compelled the Soviets to reject the proposal. Moscow especially objected to the plan's requirement that they surrender their Security Council veto. As they saw it, their veto was all that might protect them from having their own nuclear weapons program throttled by the UN. They were equally outraged by the Baruch Plan's suggestion that the international authority would only fully realize its control over American nuclear weapons *after* it established effective inspections and ownership of dangerous nuclear activities in the Soviet Union.[21]

The United States, however, was hardly in a compromising mood. Because they were convinced of nuclear weapons' offensive strategic value and enjoyed a nuclear monopoly in 1945, most U.S. officials were not about to forego the bomb without the controls and sanctions called for in the Baruch Plan.[22] For the same reasons, the Soviets were convinced that acquiring nuclear weapons was imperative and that the plan was not in their interest. As such, UN nuclear negotiations quickly reached an impasse.[23]

A question worth asking over a half century after the Baruch Plan's demise is just how sound its key assumptions were. There is little question that the Baruch Plan was correct in arguing that nuclear weapons favored the aggressor. Far less convincing today, however, is the notion that a nation's first use of such weapons automatically guarantees victory. In fact, nations are unlikely to use nuclear weapons unless they are convinced that their targeted opponent will not strike back. Guaranteeing this, however, requires confidence that one can knock out most, if not all, of an opponent's strategic weapons force. If nations can ensure that their strategic forces can survive a first strike, then a modicum of deterrence is possible even if more than one nation possesses strategic weapons. Such a "balance" is hardly automatic: It requires great effort to maintain strategic forces that will be reliable, survivable, controllable, and effective under all contingencies.[24] But it is more or less achievable, which suggests that the Baruch Plan's authors overplayed their hand in arguing that there was *no* protection against a nuclear aggressor.

In part, this distorted vision of nuclear war was simply a reflection of America's nuclear monopoly and how the United States conducted strategic bombing against Germany and Japan after it had run out of military targets.[25] Thus, the emphasis in the Acheson-Lilienthal Report on "the really revolutionary character of these weapons, particularly as weapons of strategic bombardment aimed at the destruction of enemy cities and the eradication of their population" was misplaced.[26] This was nominally true, but only so long as nuclear weapons were only possessed by the United States. The report, however, argued that this would remain the case even *after* these weapons proliferated. Anxious to promote international atomic controls as a policy imperative, America's atomic scientists de-emphasized the value of retaliation. As the Jeffries Report noted:

The most that an independent American nucleonic rearmament can achieve is the certainty that a sudden total devastation of New York or Chicago can be answered the next day by an even more extensive devastation of the cities of the aggressor and the hope that the fear of such a retaliation will paralyze the aggressor. The whole history of mankind teaches that this is a very uncertain hope, and that accumulated weapons of destruction "go off" sooner or later, even if this means a senseless mutual destruction.[27]

Perhaps, but more than a half century of effort at nuclear superpower deterrence, competition, and nuclear weapons nonuse suggests otherwise. Moreover, this point was not beyond the imagination of those reflecting on these issues in 1945. Even then, critical arguments were being made publicly against the assumption that "under atomic warfare there would be a new and tremendous advantage in being first to attack."[28]

It is interesting to speculate what might have happened if the idea of nuclear deterrence had been more popular in 1945 and 1946. It would be naive to assume that it would have prompted the Soviets to accept the Baruch Plan. Stalin, after all, had a crash nuclear weapons program of his own and had announced his intention to rearm against the West before a vast "election" audience in February 1946.[29] But it is likely that it would have allowed a much more fulsome debate over the plan and made it politically much more costly for Moscow to summarily reject it.

Indeed, U.S. and Soviet officials would have been under far less pressure to seek immediate, absolute advantage regarding America's temporary nuclear monopoly were they not so seized with fears that nuclear first use guaranteed victory. Certainly, discussion and debate over the specifics of atomic energy control, including consideration of other ways to implement some of the Baruch Plan's tougher provisions, would have been far more likely. Nor would there have been so great a temptation to oversell the inherent safety and potential economic benefits of nuclear power and denaturing.

With the Soviet rejection of the plan in December 1946, though, even the soundest aspects of the Baruch Plan were abandoned. The plan and its supporters presumed apocalyptic failure, that is, total nuclear war if the plan was not adopted immediately in its entirety or if any nation (such as the Soviet Union) merely acquired nuclear weapons.[30] In this they were clearly proved wrong by the Soviets' test of a nuclear device in 1949 and the advent of the Korean War. Then, too, by the end of 1946, Churchill's warnings against entrusting "the secret knowledge or experience of the atomic bomb" to the UN in the face of Stalin's expansionism began to take root within the U.S. government.[31] By 1950, few U.S. officials thought the Baruch Plan was actionable.

Indeed, it would take nearly three decades and India's 1974 test of a "peaceful" nuclear explosive before the Baruch Plan's concerns about timely warning, condign punishment, and the dangerous character of certain portions of the civilian nuclear cycle would again become "hot" topics for U.S. policy makers. In 1976, though, Congress was outraged when it learned that U.S. nuclear exports and assistance were directly involved in the production of India's first nuclear explosive. In reaction, it tightened U.S. nuclear export controls in 1978 and demanded that no U.S. nuclear assistance be given unless it could be safeguarded against diversion using the stiff criteria of timely warning. By then, however, considerable damage had already been done. With the nuclear sharing launched under President Eisenhower, fissionable material production technology had been spread worldwide, a weak system of nuclear inspections had been established, and the peaceful nuclear world hoped for under the Baruch Plan was made even more remote.

NOTES

1. See Alice Kimball Smith, *A Peril and a Hope: The Scientists' Movement in America, 1945–47* (Chicago: University of Chicago Press, 1965), v.

2. Ibid., 470.

3. "Prospectus on Nucleonics," a report submitted to Arthur H. Compton, November 18, 1944, reprinted in Smith, *A Peril and a Hope*, 552.

4. Ibid.

5. "A Report to the Secretary of War—June, 1945," *Bulletin of the Atomic Scientists* (May 1, 1946): 2–4.

6. Cf. David E. Lilienthal, *A Report on the International Control of Atomic Energy* (Washington, D.C.: USGPO, March 16, 1946), 1, and "The Baruch Plan: Statement by the United States Representative (Baruch) to the United Nations Atomic Energy Commission, June 14, 1946," reprinted in U.S. Department of State, *Documents on Disarmament, 1945–1959*, vol. 1 (Washington, D.C.: USGPO, 1960), 7.

7. Cf. "Joint Declaration by the Head of Government of the United States, the United Kingdom, and Canada, November 15, 1945," reprinted in U.S. Department of State, *Documents on Disarmament, 1945–1959*, vol. 1, 1–3; Lilienthal, *Report on International Control*, 2; and "A Report to the Secretary of War—June, 1945."

8. On these points see "A Report to the Secretary of War—June, 1945" and Louis N. Ridenour, Jr., "There Is No Defense," in *One World or None*, edited by Dexter Masters and Katherine Way (New York: McGraw-Hill, 1946), 33–38.

9. See Lilienthal, *Report on International Control*, 21.

10. Ibid., 9.

11. See Paul Leventhal, "IAEA's Safeguards Shortcomings—A Critique" (Washington, D.C.: Nuclear Control Institute, September 12, 1994), and Leonard Weiss, "The Concept of 'Timely Warning' in the Nuclear Nonproliferation Act of 1978," Minority Staff Position Paper, Senate Subcommittee on Energy, Nuclear Proliferation and Governmental Processes, April 1, 1985.

12. "The Baruch Plan," 12.

13. Ibid.

14. See Lilienthal, *Report on International Control*, 2, 17–20. For a more detailed discussion of this point see Albert Wohlstetter, et al., *Swords from Plowshares: The Military Potential of Civilian Nuclear Energy* (Chicago: University of Chicago Press, 1978), 437, 447–56.

15. See Lilienthal, *Report on International Control*, 14, 21–30.

16. See U.S. State Department, Press Release No. 235, April 9, 1946, in Lilienthal, *Report on International Control*, 1.

17. What may explain the scientists' cognitive dissonance concerning denaturing is the difference between the first-generation plutonium implosion device that the Air Force dropped on Nagasaki and the next generation implosion devices tested a year later. Given the amount of spontaneous fission that reactor-grade plutonium (Pu 240 and 242) generates, the relatively long time it took the initial Nagasaki design to implode the plutonium to criticality, the use of reactor-grade plutonium risked producing low-yield duds that would "fizzile" rather than produce a nominal (10–12 kiloton) yield. The next generation of implosion devices, however, employed a levitated pit design that was far more efficient and could

overcome reactor-grade plutonium's tendency to pre-ignite. Oppenheimer and others on the Manhattan Project knew of the possibility of the levitated pit design prior to Nagasaki but did not actually have a chance to test it until 1946. In any case, that plutonium could be "denatured" was publicly refuted some thirty years later by Robert Selden, a leading U.S. nuclear weapons engineer. In a briefing given to the International Atomic Energy Agency's safeguards staff in Geneva, Selden revealed that the United States had successfully exploded a multiple kiloton device in the early 1960s fueled entirely with high-burn-up (i.e., "denatured") power reactor plutonium. See Robert W. Selden, *Reactor Plutonium and Nuclear Explosives* (Livermore, CA: Lawrence Livermore Laboratory, 1978), and Richard Rhodes, *Dark Sun: The Making of the Hydrogen Bomb* (New York: Simon and Schuster, 1995), 188–89, 246.

18. U.S. State Department, Press Release, 3.

19. On the continued popularity and error of thinking that reactor-grade plutonium cannot be used to make nuclear weapons see Victor Gilinsky, "Restraining the Spread of Nuclear Weapons: A Walk on the Supply Side," in *Limiting Nuclear Proliferation*, edited by Jed C. Snyder and Samuel F. Wells, Jr. (Cambridge, MA: Ballinger Publishing Company, 1985), and "Plutonium from U.S.-Supplied LWRs for North Korea: Do We Have to Worry About It?" a presentation before the Forum on Prompting International Scientific, Technological and Economic Cooperation in the Korean Peninsula: Enhancing Stability and International Dialogue, Instituto Diplomatico, Rome, Italy, June 1–2, 2000, published at www.wizard.net/~npec.

20. See Lilienthal, *Report on International Control*, 44–53.

21. See "Statement by the Soviet Representative (Gromyko) to the Security Council, March 5, 1947," in U.S. Department of State, *Documents on Disarmament 1945–1959*, vol. 1, 64–82.

22. There were, however, a few that objected to Baruch's modifications of the proposal laid out in the Acheson-Lilienthal Report and more than a few U.S. atomic scientists who were wary of Baruch's interventions. See Dean Acheson, *Present at the Creation*, (New York: W. W. Norton, 1969), 154–56 and Smith, *A Peril and a Hope*, 464–71.

23. For Soviet agreement on the likely offensive use of nuclear weapons against civilian population centers see Smith, *A Peril and a Hope*, 67.

24. On these points see the classic study, Albert Wohlstetter, "The Delicate Balance of Terror," *Foreign Affairs* (January 1959): 211–34.

25. See Ronald Schaffer, "American Military Ethics in World War II: The Bombing of German Civilians," *The Journal of American History* (September 1980): 318–34, and Lawrence Freedman, "The Strategy of Hiroshima," *The Journal of Strategic Studies* (May 1978): 76–97.

26. Lilienthal, *Report on International Control*, 1. Cf. "A Report to the Secretary of War—*June, 1945*."

27. "Prospectus on Nucleonics," in Smith, *A Peril and a Hope*, 552–53.

28. See especially Jacob Viner, "The Implications of the Atomic Bomb for International Relations," Proceedings of the American Philosophical Society, November 16, 1945, reprinted in *International Economics: Studies by Jacob Viner* (Glenco, IL: The Free Press, 1951), 300–9. Similar but somewhat less coherent views were also expressed privately in 1945 by General Curtis LeMay, then dep-

3
Atoms for Peace

With the Soviets' rejection of the Baruch UN Plan in 1946 and their explosion of a nuclear device in 1949, Washington officials feared Moscow might use its nuclear force to destroy the United States. The key question was when.

Baruch had noted in his UN address that "no nation would think of starting a war with only one bomb."[1] But at what point would they? An estimate made in the Franck Report in 1945 pegged the figure at between 50 and 170 Hiroshima-sized bombs. With this many weapons, the report argued, one could prepare a "sneak attack" on the United States and hit "a large enough fraction of the nation's industry and population (500 square miles, or 100 areas of five square miles each) to make their destruction a crippling blow to the nation's war potential."[2]

Shortly after the Soviets exploded their first device, the National Security Council (NSC) updated this analysis, factoring in the probable inaccuracy of Soviet bomb delivery. Again, using the destruction of 100 major American cities as the threshold, the NSC estimated that when the Soviets acquired 200 nominal bombs—which they estimated would be by mid-1954—the Soviets would have enough weapons to launch a surprise attack capable of seriously "damaging" the United States.[3]

ADDRESSING THE "CRITICAL DATE"

Time, it seemed, was running out. With each passing month, the NSC noted, Soviet nuclear production would increase and bring Moscow closer to the date when it might "calculate that it [had] a sufficient atomic capability to make a surprise attack on us, nullifying our atomic superiority and creating a military situation decisively in its favor."[4] Although, with the massive U.S. nuclear build-up that attended the Korean War, U.S. Air Force officials seemed confident that they could pre-empt any planned Soviet air strike, their civilian masters were not so sure.[5] In 1952 (two years before the predicted "critical date" when the Soviets were projected to acquire 200 nuclear weapons), President Harry Truman established a panel of consultants on disarmament to review the bidding. Chaired by J. Robert Oppenheimer, this panel once more sounded the alarm:

If the atomic arms race continues . . . we seem likely to have within a relatively few years a situation in which the two great powers will each have a clear-cut capacity to do very great damage to the other, while each will be unable to exert that capacity except at the gravest risk of receiving similar terrible blows in return. And this situation is likely to be largely unaffected by the fact that one side may always have many more weapons than the other. There is likely to be a point in our time when the Soviet Union has "enough" bombs, no matter how many more we ourselves may have.[6]

This was hardly good news. In fact, the panel was forecasting nearly the opposite of the kind of mutual nuclear deterrence celebrated today. Instead of the Soviets being deterred from attacking the United States for fear of being retaliated against after launching an attack, the panel argued that the Soviet Union would soon acquire the capability to so damage the United States that it might well be tempted to strike. Under these conditions, both sides would have an *increased* incentive to pre-empt the other. Deterrence, to the extent it was possible, would rest on the frightfully slender (and unlikely) reed of both sides being convinced that the other could quickly detect and effectively pre-empt the other's preparations for war.[7] The good news, however, was the panel's generous estimate of when the Soviets might acquire such a "knockout blow" capability. Factoring in "careful" defense planning, the panel estimated that the Soviets might be able to "destroy our economy beyond recovery" in a "few years" with as few as 600 40-kiloton bombs. With development of a U.S. continental air defense (then being debated), though, the number required, in the panel's view, could rise as high as 15,000 weapons, a number "not out of reach" for the Soviets "within the next decade" (i.e., sometime in the 1960s).[8]

In any case, the panel believed that public candor about the approaching nuclear threat was necessary to facilitate needed restraint. It recommended that the number of atomic weapons and bombers in our arsenal, a rough estimate of the rate of U.S. fissile materials production, and our estimates of Soviet nuclear strength be released. This was essential, the panel argued, to ensure that neither side would be tempted to launch a preventive war "before it is too late only to find out that the time for such a blow already passed."

Beyond such public diplomacy and strengthening of U.S. active air defenses, the panel also recommended limited arms control. Trying to eliminate all nuclear weapons through international controls might not be feasible, but in the panel's view this was not necessary. To eliminate the real nuclear danger, the ability of nations to "strike each other [with] direct and crippling blows," all one needed was to "get a reduction in the size of stockpiles . . . such that neither side need fear a sudden knock-out from the other." This "would not give assurance against the use of atomic weapons," but would at least protect against the danger of "a surprise knockout blow."[9]

Acting on these recommendations seemed critical. Yet, by the time the panel had completed its report in late 1952, a new administration had been voted into office. To ensure that the panel's views were heard, Oppenheimer worked throughout January and February 1953 on an article for *Foreign Affairs*. When he went in March to Eisenhower's advisers to secure permission to publish his piece, he was asked to brief the new NSC staff and the president's psychological warfare advisor, C. D. Jackson. Two of the panel's recommendations were acted upon almost immediately. Jackson and a small group of top officials were assigned to come up with a series of speeches on the approaching nuclear crisis, and Eisenhower decided to propose mutual military fissile stockpile reductions to the Soviets in an upcoming speech.[10]

The stockpile idea, however, could not be thoroughly staffed and ended up as no more than a passage in a speech to the American Society of Newspaper Editors on April 16, 1953. Eisenhower proposed to slow U.S. military fissile production if the Soviets agreed to resolve a list of outstanding East-West issues. Although the Soviets' UN representative, Andrei Vishinsky, found it "interesting," there was no specific Soviet follow-up.[11]

Meanwhile, the White House's speech writing effort on the coming atomic crisis, dubbed Operation Candor, continued. By July, several speech drafts had been written but were rejected by Jackson and others as being too horrific.[12] Lacking any clear direction as to how to brighten these drafts, Jackson had about given up on the project when news came that the Soviets had just tested their first thermonuclear, or "boosted," device. This news, upsetting in itself, was even more disturbing in light of the Panel of Consultants Report, which had merely assumed a growing Soviet stockpile of crude 40-kiloton fission bombs.[13] Now, as Atomic Energy Commission Chairman Lewis Strauss publicly noted, a single thermonuclear bomb could destroy all of New York City.

Eisenhower, vacationing at his Denver retreat, was dismayed. As he explained in a top-secret memorandum to Secretary of State John Foster Dulles, Operation Candor was now critical to bring the coming arms crisis to a head. Once the crisis was explained publicly and the Soviets still refused to agree to international atomic control, he argued, Americans could assume that Moscow intended aggression. Under these circumstances, he worried that the United States "would have to be constantly ready, in an instantaneous basis, to inflict greater loss upon the enemy than he could reasonably hope to inflict on us." Beyond possibly developing a pre-emptive strike option that might be triggered by the first signs of a Soviet strike, Eisenhower warned Dulles that "we would be forced to consider whether or not our duty to future generations did not require us to initiate war at the most propitious moment that *we* [emphasis added] could designate."[14]

EISENHOWER'S IDEA

It was at this point that Eisenhower wrote that he began "to search around for any kind of idea that could bring the world to look at the atomic problem in a broad and intelligent way and still escape the impasse to action created by Russia's intransigence in the matter of mutual or neutral inspection of resources."[15] Returning to Washington to be briefed on new disarmament proposals the United States might present before the UN in the fall, Eisenhower shared his thoughts with his special assistant for national security affairs, Robert Cutler: What if the superpowers contributed "X amount" of fissile material for "peaceful" purposes, the amount X being a figure the U.S. could handle from its stockpile but that would be difficult for the Soviets to match?[16]

Eisenhower's hope was not only to eliminate the Soviets' ability to knock out the United States but to avoid the difficult negotiating issue of establishing a comprehensive intrusive inspection system first, a problem that stymied the Baruch Plan.[17] Yet, initially Eisenhower's disarmament scheme met with resistance. Both Jackson and Atomic Energy Commissioner Lewis Strauss worried that the plan might backfire with the United States giving too much material and the Soviets too little. Also, they feared that the plan would be of less value several years on, when true fusion weapons replaced existing fissile devices in both U.S. and Soviet stockpiles. President Eisenhower, though, believed his idea deserved more study and asked both Jackson and Strauss to reconsider. What followed was a gradual reversal of Jackson's and Strauss' views and a major reworking of the idea into a gradual, incremental approach toward atomic disarmament.[18]

Reporting back to the president by memo on November 6, Strauss argued that the pooling idea might make sense as a first step toward atomic arms control. Here Strauss's reasoning was drawn almost directly from the Panel of Consultants' earlier assessment of the Soviet threat:

If it could be agreed that as a preliminary step to total disarmament, both parties would in the first instance retain a minimum number of atomic weapons as a means of retaliating against aggressions (but not enough to mount an annihilating surprise attack) . . . it would represent progress in that the threat of war would then be reduced to a degree of injury that could be absorbed without total destruction. The incentive to Russia to attack would be diminished by inability to make such an attack overwhelming and decisive.

All of this was realizable, Strauss argued, if (1) fissile contributions to the international pool could be steadily increased over time, (2) sufficient confidence could be built to close down all military fissile production plants and restrict mining and refining of uranium and thorium to existing facilities, and (3) Strauss's own plan of guarding the contributed fissile against theft (dilution of the material in large, remote, underground tanks) was adopted.[19]

With greater demand for contributed fissile material for civilian atomic applications, Strauss reasoned that even greater weapons stockpile reductions would have to be made. This, in turn, would reduce the Soviet military threat and make genuine East-West trust more likely. The plan in its most advanced form (with a military fissile production cut-off) also had the advantage of not requiring international ownership (a Baruch measure that the Soviets opposed) and only limited inspections. Thus, as Jackson, Dulles, Eisenhower, and Strauss later explained it, the plan could well lead to atomic disarmament even though its initial dimensions would be quite modest.[20]

Unfortunately, lost in all of this concern about drawing down Soviet and U.S. arsenals and fissile production was the danger of horizontal proliferation. The essentials of Strauss's memo (including his dilution idea to prevent contributed material from being seized) were, in fact, reflected in President Eisenhower's address to the UN on December 8, 1953. But Eisenhower focused his comments on reducing the danger of superpower nuclear rivalry, not on slowing the spread of nuclear weapons to smaller states.

Eisenhower explained that joint contributions of fissionable materials would be made to the UN International Atomic Energy Agency (IAEA). He also noted that the agency would store and protect the material against surprise seizures and "devise methods whereby this fissionable material would be allocated to serve the peaceful purposes of mankind."[21] But there was no explanation as to how the IAEA might prevent the reactors and related technology it was to share with the world's nonweapons states from being used to produce nuclear weapons-usable materials.

At first, such inattention might have been excusable since, as administration officials later explained, the draw-down of U.S. and Soviet stockpiles through contributions to the IAEA would only become significant when nuclear power plants were built abroad in large numbers beginning in the early 1960s. Also, shortly after the president's UN address, State and Defense Department officials debated whether or not Eisenhower's proposal meant that the United States was ready to negotiate nuclear disarmament immediately. The answer, as clarified at a top-level White House meeting January 6, 1954, was "no." Secretary of State Dulles thought that even under the best of circumstances the president's plan was unlikely to produce major disarmament for at least another five years; Eisenhower speculated it could conceivably take another forty.[22]

THE LOGICAL PROJECTION AND FOLLOW-THROUGH

Still, early in 1954 U.S. officials had given only cursory consideration to how the international agency the president had proposed might prevent the military diversion of the "peaceful" nuclear technology. The study group assigned to detail the proposal agreed that the agency should have this goal but was silent on how it might go about this. Certainly, no one opposed having the agency safeguard the materials it allocated to civilian projects. However, it was argued that the key advantage of having the agency do this was not so much to prevent the military diversion of such technology to other nations as it was to gain the experience necessary to administer an end to U.S.-Soviet military nuclear production.[23]

This preoccupation with curbing vertical proliferation continued even after U.S. officials privately briefed the Soviets, who objected to Eisenhower's proposal on the grounds that the international sharing of nuclear power technology would only increase the world's ability to make bombs.[24] Even later, in 1954 and 1955 when the State Department Policy Planning staff and the Atomic Energy Commission seriously considered what sort of safeguards the program's proposed international agency should impose to prevent military diversions, their recommendations were eclipsed by Eisenhower's original concern with curbing the vertical growth of Soviet fissile stockpiles.

In fact, the safeguard suggestions they made for the proposed agency included a number of sound ideas. These included preventing nations from keeping significant amounts of spent reactor fuel (which contained weapons-usable plutonium), conducting all reprocessing and enrichment in regional parks, safeguarding fertile materials (natural and depleted uranium) that might be irradiated to make fissile, and requiring recipients of agency nuclear assistance to place all of their nuclear activities under agency safeguards.[25]

Unfortunately, none of these ideas survived in IAEA statute negotiations. U.S. Ambassador James Wadsworth, the U.S. representative to these talks, pleaded for vigorous agency controls over fertile materials, reactor by-products, and over any move toward the separation of plutonium. He even got language for such controls incorporated into a draft of the agency's statute.[26] After opposition to these provisions from India, France, the Soviet Union, and Switzerland, though, negotiations over the agency's creation reached an impasse. Wadsworth requested forty-eight hours for consultations and after a series of conferences with Secretary of State Dulles and Strauss was instructed to give in.[27] Although Wadsworth expressed the hope that the IAEA would later reconsider these issues, abandoning these provisions was necessary, it was argued, since without continued political progress in establishing the IAEA, the entire architecture of the larger Atoms for Peace U.S.-Soviet fissile reduction scheme would collapse.[28] Also, the world's smaller nations were so excited about the prospects of exploiting nuclear energy's peaceful applications that tremendous pressure was placed on the United States and other nations to proceed.[29]

This setback was hardly noticed in Washington. Instead, throughout 1956, President Eisenhower was busy promoting a U.S.-Soviet military fissile production cut-off treaty under which the IAEA might assume custody of the fissile material already produced and verify the agreement.[30] Based on an internal disarmament inspections study, the United States formally proposed this idea at the UN in 1956 and continued to promote it through 1958 as "the logical projection and follow-through" of the Atoms for Peace proposal.[31] Again, as before, the focus was on reducing the prospect of the Soviets or of any other nation acquiring a knockout blow stockpile. As Secretary of State Dulles explained to Congress, the best way to deter nuclear weapons states from using the weapons they had was to make sure they transferred enough fissile material so they would not have a stockpile large enough to launch the "completely devastating attack" necessary to defeat America's superior mobilization base.[32]

SHY OF "100 PERCENT PERFECTION"

Unfortunately, this emphasis on reducing massive stockpiles did little to strengthen IAEA safeguards. In fact, the proposed safeguard procedures, which were lifted directly from the president's internal disarmament inspections study, were basic. Throughout 1957 and 1958, U.S. government disarmament experts testified before the Senate freely admitting that none of the proposed safeguards were likely to detect a military diversion until *after* it was completed. They also conceded that the proposed procedures for safeguarding nuclear fuel production facilities (e.g., uranium enrichment plants, plutonium reprocessing facilities, and nuclear fuel fabrication plants) were unlikely to account for as much as 10 percent of their production of weapons-usable materials (numerous bombs' worth a year) and that for power reactors 2 percent of the spent fuel (containing many weapons' worth of unseparated plutonium) was likely to go unaccounted for.[33]

None of these deficiencies, however, was considered to be fatal. Several bombs' worth of material might get by the inspectors, it was argued, but it would not matter. As the chairman of the Joint Chiefs, both secretaries of Defense and State, and the president's own disarmament advisor made clear in public testimony: Only if a nation amassed a vast stockpile of weapons, an arsenal massive enough to knock out the United States and its key industries, could it ever pose an effective nuclear threat.[34] Foolproof safeguards that could afford timely warning of even one or several bombs' worth of material being diverted, then, were simply deemed to be unnecessary, since only large, continuous diversions could provide a nation with material sufficient for a truly threatening force.[35] Thus, as U.S. UN Ambassador Harold Stassen noted in explaining the "substance" of Atoms for Peace before the UN in 1957, "it would be perfectly possible, even under the most effective controls, for some ... future government ... to take away and divert without the knowledge of the inspectors, a quantity of fissionable material from which twenty, forty or even fifty multi-megaton bombs could be fabricated." But having "100 percent perfection of inspection or of accountability" to prevent this, he explained, was neither possible nor necessary since as

long as there does exist on various sides in the world a remaining nuclear weapons capability, there would not be the incentive for relatively minor diversion into unauthorized weapons. Nor would there be the terrible consequences if there were relatively minor diversions for a few weapons; because those few weapons would be restrained, canceled out and deterred by the remaining capability in the hands of nations on various sides.[36]

All of this thinking, of course, was quite consistent with the president's original rationale for Atoms for Peace. Unfortunately, virtually all of it, including its preoccupation with knockout blows, was wrong. Certainly, prior to 1945, America's ability to strike back effectively at overseas aggressors required that it have a secure military industrial base. But the advent of air-atomic forces in the 1950s changed this. Now, with Soviet and U.S. nuclear bombers on the ready, the most urgent strategic targets were no longer either nation's key military-industrial sites—as Eisenhower and those closest to him believed—but both sides' nuclear bombers and bases.

This last point was one that the U.S. Air Force only began to fully grapple with in the early 1950s. In fact, as a series of Air Force-sponsored studies made clear, U.S. air bases were much more vulnerable to attack in the early 1950s than was generally assumed. Rather than hundreds or thousands of bombs (the massive sort of knockout blow arsenal that Atoms for Peace was directed against), analysts calculated that merely scores of weapons targeted against our nuclear bombers could have destroyed them and their bases and left America defenseless. Taking up these experts' recommendations, the Air Force was able gradually to reduce these vulnerabilities in the mid and late 1950s. Resolving these issues rather than those for Atoms for Peace, significantly reduced the likelihood of war.[37]

More important, given Atoms for Peace's preoccupation with preventing nations from amassing *large* stockpiles, the program did little to address the prospect of horizontal accidental or catalytic nuclear wars. In fact, with the further spread of nuclear weapons to other nations, the major nuclear powers might be drawn into a nuclear war by a smaller nation's use of only one or a few nuclear devices. Yet, Atoms for Peace, with its promotion of nuclear transfers and loose safeguards, made the acquisition of such capabilities *more* likely. The program understood that the superpowers' strategic arms build-up jeopardized the prospect for peace. It also recognized that curbing these arsenals' growth and the spread of strategic weapons were related tasks. What it failed to grasp, unfortunately, was how best to achieve these tasks.

In fact, three years after Eisenhower announced Atoms for Peace, both U.S. UN Ambassador Henry Cabot Lodge and Ambassador Wadsworth conceded this possibility when they publicly admitted that the proliferation of even one nuclear weapon could "easily ignite a nuclear conflagration" and that the controls initially afforded the IAEA were insufficient to prevent this threat.[38] Indeed, by the late 1950s, there was reason to worry that Eisenhower's Atoms for Peace program and the nuclear technology it was spreading were creating problems, not solutions, and that some new way to prevent proliferation would be necessary.

NOTES

1. "The Baruch Plan: Statement by the United States Representative (Baruch) to the United Nations Atomic Energy Commission, June 14, 1946," reprinted in U.S. Department of State, *Documents on Disarmament, 1945–1959*, vol. 1 (Washington, DC: USGPO, 1960), 12.

2. "Prospectus on Nucleonics," in Smith, *A Peril and a Hope: The Scientists' Movement in America, 1945–47* (Chicago: University of Chicago Press, 1965), 564.

3. "National Security Council Memorandum 68," April 7, 1950, reprinted in U.S. Department of State, *The Foreign Relations of the United States, Diplomatic Papers, 1950*, vol. I: *National Security Affairs* (Washington, D.C. USGPO, 1977), 265.

4. Ibid.

5. See the detailed accounting of the debate concerning pre-emption and preventative war during this period in Scott D. Sagan and Kenneth N. Waltz, *The Spread of Nuclear Weapons* (New York: W. W. Norton, 1995), 57–61, and the extensive discussion regarding U.S. Strategic Air Command's plans for an overwhelming pre-emptive air nuclear strike against Russia and its view that it would have up to a month of warning of a Soviet nuclear strike in Richard Rhodes, *Dark Sun* (New York: Simon and Schuster, 1995), 561–64; David Alan Rosenberg, "A Smoking, Radiation Ruin at the End of Two Hours," *International Security* (Winter 1981–1982) 3–17; and "The Origins of Overkill: Nuclear Weapons and American Strategy, 1945–1960," *International Security* 7, no. 4 (Spring 1983): 3–71.

6. U.S. Department of State, "Armaments and American Policy: A Report of the Panel of Consultants on Disarmament to the Department of State," State Department Archives, file number 330.13/1–1553, January 15, 1953.

7. For a discussion and historiography on this point, see Rhodes, *Dark Sun*, 528–29.

8. See U.S. Department of State, "Armaments and American Policy."

9. Ibid.

10. See J. Robert Oppenheimer, "Atomic Weapons and American Policy," *Foreign Affairs* 31, no. 4; (Summer 1953): 525–535, and U.S. Atomic Energy Commission, *In the Matter of J. Robert Oppenheimer: Transcript of Hearings Before Personnel Security Board, April 12, 1954, Through May 6, 1954* (Washington, D.C.: USGPO, 1954), 96.

11. See "Text of Speech by Eisenhower Outlining Proposal for Peace in World," *New York Times*, April 17, 1953, p. 4; "Dulles Bids Soviets Cooperate or Face Vast West Arming." *New York Times*, April 18, 1953, p. 1; "Text of the Soviet Union's Statement Replying to President Eisenhower's Speech," *New York Times*, April 26, 1953, p. 64.

12. See "Memorandum from Operation Candor to President Eisenhower, July 8, 1953," Masterson Files, *Eisenhower Papers*, reprinted in Robert Bryan and Lawrence H. Larsen, *The Eisenhower Administration 1953–1961: A Documentary History* (New York: Random House, 1974), 188–94; and "Chronology—Candor—Wheaties, September 30, 1954," confidential, *Jackson Papers*, Box "24" *Time Inc.* file, Atoms for Peace Evolution (1).

13. See John Lear, "Ike and the Peaceful Atom," *The Reporter*, January 12, 1956, 12; and Lewis Strauss, *Men and Decisions* (Garden City, NY: Doubleday, 1962), 346–47.

14. See "Memorandum by the President to the Secretary of State, September 8, 1953," in *Foreign Relations of the United States, 1952–54*, Vol. 2 (Washington, D.C.: USGPO, 1990), 461.

15. See Dwight D. Eisenhower, *Mandate for Change* (Garden City, NY: Doubleday, 1963), 252.

16. See Memorandum for Admiral Strauss, C. D. Jackson from Robert Cutler, September 10, 1953, Top Secret, in *Eisenhower: Papers as President 1953–61*, Ann Whitman File, Administration Series, Box "5," Atoms for Peace Folder, Eisenhower Library, declassified in 1977; "Chronology—Candor—Wheaties," September, 30, 1954; and Memorandum for Files, February 3, 1956, *Jackson Papers*, Box "24," *Time Inc.* File, Atoms for Peace Evolution (2).

17. See Thomas F. Soapes, "A Cold Warrior Seeks Peace: Eisenhower's Strategy for Nuclear Disarmament," *Diplomatic History* (Winter 1979–1980): 65.

18. See Memorandum for the President from Lewis Strauss, September 17, 1953, Secret, *Eisenhower: Papers as President*, Ann Whitman File, Administration Series, Box "5," Atoms for Peace Folder, declassified in 1978; Strauss, *Men and Decisions*, 347–63; Corbin Allardice and Edward Trapnell, *The Atomic Energy Commission* (New York: Praeger Publishers, 1974), 199, 201; and Sherman Adams, *Firsthand Report* (New York: Harper and Brothers, 1961), 112, 118.

19. See Memorandum for C. D. Jackson from Lewis Strauss with draft attached, November 6, 1953, *Jackson Papers*, Box "25," *Time Inc.* File, Atoms for Peace Evolution (3).

20. See C. D. Jackson's log entries of November 17, 20, 25, 27, and 30, 1953; Jackson Papers, Box "56," *Time Inc.* File, Atoms for Peace Evolution (3). "President Wants U.S. to Lift Curb on Sharing Atom Data," *New York Times*, December 17, 1953, A1, "Dulles Holds U.S. Is Ready to Discuss Ban on Atomic War," *New York Times*, December 23, 1953, A1, "West to Accept Soviets' Proposal to Delay Meeting," *New York Times*, December 29, 1953, A1; and Memorandum of Conversation, Bermuda Meeting, Restricted Session of Heads of Government, December 4, 1953, Top Secret, *Eisenhower: Papers as President*, Ann Whitman File, International Meetings Series, Box "1," Folder: Bermuda-State Department Report, Eisenhower Library, declassified in 1976, 2, 4, and 6.

21. "United States 'Atoms for Peace' Proposal: Address by President Eisenhower to the General Assembly, December 8, 1953," in U.S. Department of State, *Documents on Disarmament, 1945–59*, vol. 2, 399.

22. See "Summary of Meeting with the Secretary of State on Implementation of the President's December 8th Speech, 6 January 1954," Top Secret, *White House Central File*, Confidential file, Box "13" folder: Candor and United Nations Speech 12/8/53 (26); Atomic Energy Commission (AEC) staff memorandum, "Review of Technical Aspects Involved in the Problem of International Control of Atomic Energy," with cover letter to Robert Bowie, from John A. Hall, November 2, 1954; "Summary of Meeting, 6 January 1954," "Summary of Meeting in the White House between President, Dulles, Strauss, et al. re Nuclear Disarmament" and President's December 8th Speech, January 16, 1954, Top Secret, *White House Central Files*, Confidential File, Boxes "12 and 13" Candor and UN Speech 12/8/53: (26) and (4) respectively, declassified in 1979; and Soapes, "Cold Warrior," 70.

23. See "A Suggested Basis for a Plan to Carry Out the President's Proposal, 'Atomic Power for Peace,' " January 13, 1954, Secret, *White House Central Files*, Confidential file, Box "13" Folder: Candor and the United Nations' Speech, 12/8/53, declassified in 1979; and U.S. Congress, Joint Committee on Atomic Energy, *Review of the International Atomic Policies and Programs of the United States*, by Robert McKinney, Joint Committee Print (Washington, D.C.: USGPO, 1960), 55–59, 66–67.

24. For the final U.S. staff plan to implement President Eisenhower's proposal submitted to the Soviets in private negotiations on March 19, 1954, and the thirty other diplomatic notes exchanged with the Soviets concerning the proposed international atomic energy agency from January 11, 1954, through September 24, 1956, see U.S. Department of State, *The U.S. Department of State Bulletin*, October 4, 1954, 478 ff. and October 22, 1956, 620–31.

25. See U.S. Atomic Energy Agency Staff Memorandum, "Review of Technical Aspects Involved in the Problem of International Control of Atomic Energy" with cover letter to Robert Bowie from John A. Hall, November 2, 1954, declassified in 1977, copy obtained through Arthur Steiner of Pan Heuristics from ERDA Historical Branch Director, Richard G. Hewlett and the U.S. Atomic Energy Commission, 751/41, December 30, 1955, U.S. Department of Energy Archives, Annex 1 to Appendix "B," "A Proposal for Averting Dangers in the Atoms-for-Peace Program."

26. See the comments of Ambassador James Wadsworth before the Conference on the Statute of the IAEA, September 24 and October 15, 1956, and his address before the Nuclear Energy Writers Association May 9, 1956, reprinted in U.S. Department of State, *State Department Bulletin*, May 28, October 8, and November 19, 1956, 539, 816–19, 900–2.

27. See Bernard B. Bechhoefer, "Negotiating the IAEA," in Bernard Bechhoefer, ed., *Postwar Negotiations for Arms Control* (Washington, D.C.: The Brookings Institution, 1961), 156–65.

28. See Wadsworth's comments cited in *State Department Bulletin*, in note 26 and Bechhoefer, "Negotiating the IAEA," 153–54.

29. See the IAEA Statute Conference Debates of the fall of 1956, particularly IAEA/CS/OR.35, 71–72 and IAEA/CS/OR. 37, 21–22; Bertrand Goldschmidt, "The Origins of the International Atomic Energy Agency," *International Atomic Energy Agency Bulletin*, (August 1977): 18–19; and Gilinsky, "Restraining the Spread of Nuclear Weapons: A Walk on the Supply Side," in Jed C. Snyder and Samuel F. Wells, Jr., eds., *Limiting Nuclear Proliferation* (Cambridge, MA: Ballinger Publishing Co., 1985), 258–59.

30. See "Letter from President Eisenhower to the Soviet Premier (Bulganin)," March 1, 1956; "United States Summary Memorandum Submitted to the Disarmament Subcommittee," May 3, 1956; "Statement by the U.S. Representative (Lodge) before the Disarmament Commission," July 3, 1956; and "Letter from President Eisenhower to the Soviet Premier (Bulganin)," August 4, 1956, in U.S. Department of State, *Documents on Disarmament 1945–59*, 593–95, 623–24, 649–50, 686.

31. See "United States Memorandum Submitted to the First Committee of the General Assembly," January 12, 1957; "Statement by the United States Representative (Stassen) to the Disarmament Subcommittee: Nuclear Weapons and Testing," March 20, 1957; "Radio and Television Address by Secretary of State Dulles," July 22, 1957; "Letter from President Eisenhower to the Soviet Premier (Bulganin)," January 12, 1958; and "Letter from President Eisenhower to the Soviet Premier (Khrushchev) on Nuclear Tests," April 8, 1958, documents 151, 161, 169, 175, 185, 197, 213, 240 and 254 in U.S. Department of State, *Documents on Disarmament 1945–1959*, vol. 2, 713–32, 763–68, 825–34, 938–39, 983–85.

32. See Dulles's Testimony of February 29, 1956, in U.S. Congress, Senate,

Committee on Foreign Relations, *Control and Reduction of Armaments*, Hearings, before a Subcommittee of the Committee on Foreign Relations on S. Res. 93, 84th Cong., 1956, pp. 60–61.

33. See, for example, U.S. Senate Committee on Foreign Relations, *Statute of the International Atomic Energy Agency, Hearings Before the Committee on Foreign Relations and Senate Members of the Joint Committee on Atomic Energy, Senate on Executive 1*, 85th Cong., 1st sess., 1957, pp. 99–100, 181–82, and "Testimony of Dr. Spofford G. English before the Senate Subcommittee on Disarmament (Extracts)," March 12, 1958, document 246 in U.S. Department of State, *Documents on Disarmament 1945–1959*, vol. 2, 956, 959, and 961.

34. For each of these top officials' reiterations of this argument, see their separate testimonies in U.S. Congress, Senate, Committee on Foreign Relations, *Control and Reduction of Armaments, Hearings*, before a Subcommittee on Foreign Relations on S. Res. 93, 84th Cong., 1956, pp. 60–61, 64–65, 68–69, 178; the testimony of Ambassador Stassen in the U.S. Senate, *Statute of the IAEA*, 15, 52, 62–63, 80, 107, 136; and "Radio and Television Address by Secretary Dulles, July 22, 1957," reprinted in U.S. Department of State, *Documents on Disarmament*, vol. 2, 825–34; and U.S. Congress, Joint Committee on Atomic Energy, *Review of the International Atomic Policies and Programs of the United States*, by Robert McKinney, Joint Committee Print (Washington, D.C.: USGPO, 1960), 780 ff.

35. See e.g., U.S. Senate, *Statute of the IAEA*, 99–100, 181–82.

36. See "Statement by the United States Representative (Stassen) to the Disarmament Subcommittee: Nuclear Weapons and Testing, March 20, 1957," in U.S. Department of State, *Documents on Disarmament 1945–1959*, vol. 2, 765–68.

37. See A. J. Wohlstetter, F. S. Hoffman, R. J. Lutz, and H. S. Rowen, *Selection and Use of Strategic Air Bases* (Santa Monica, CA: The RAND Corporation, R-266, April 1954); Bruce Smith, *The RAND Corporation* (Cambridge: Harvard University Press, 1966), 195–240; and Fred Kaplan, *The Wizards of Armageddon* (New York: Simon and Schuster, 1983), 99–102, 120–21.

38. See "Statement by the United States Representative (Lodge) to the Disarmament Commission, July 3, 1956," in U.S. Department of State, *Documents on Disarmament 1945–1959*, vol. 2, 649, and the comments of Ambassador James Wadsworth of October 15, 1956, before the Conference on the Statute of the IAEA, reprinted in U.S. Department of State, *State Bulletin*, May 28, 1956, 898–902.

4

The Nuclear
Nonproliferation Treaty

It is easy to confuse American efforts to promote negotiation of the Nuclear Nonproliferation Treaty (NPT) with the Atoms for Peace Program. Both efforts encouraged nuclear technology transfers and international atomic energy safeguards over such assistance. Both called on nations to abandon efforts to acquire nuclear weapons.[1]

Yet what distinguishes these nonproliferation initiatives from one another—their different views of what strategic developments were most worrisome—is far more important than any similarity between the two. Indeed, it is only by understanding how different each of these nonproliferation initiatives' strategic concerns are that we can appreciate what is uniquely sound and deficient about each. Where the Atoms for Peace Program was geared to reduce the threat supposedly posed by arsenals large enough to destroy most of America's major cities, the NPT was directed against catalytic and accidental nuclear wars that could arise either from the further spread of nuclear weapons or from the build-up of the superpowers' arsenals. Unfortunately, because neither initiative focused sufficiently on the most serious proliferation challenges, neither ultimately promoted effective safeguards against the proliferation threats that are now emerging.

Besides helping to distinguish the NPT from Atoms for Peace, though, understanding the NPT's premises is also critical to understanding the treaty itself. Indeed, without an understanding of how these premises helped generate the treaty's key provisions and how these premises changed during the treaty's negotiation, one is confronted with a pact that appears to be at odds with itself. In fact, those who first backed the treaty's negotiation were primarily concerned with how horizontal proliferation (i.e., the spread of nuclear weapons to other nations) might intentionally or accidentally spark (or catalyze) nuclear wars between the superpowers or smaller states. This gave rise to the treaty's prohibitions and safeguards against sharing or accepting nuclear weapons or nuclear weapons technology (Articles I, II, and III of the NPT).

A decade later, however, when the treaty's negotiation was nearly complete, this was not the key concern. Instead, most of the treaty's negotiators were preoccupied with how growing vertical proliferation (the quantitative and qualitative improvement of the superpowers' strategic arsenals) might lead to unauthorized or accidental nuclear wars and prompt other nations to go nuclear. They believed any nation might deter another with a small, finite number of nuclear weapons but believed that all nations would be better off if they foreswore nuclear arms and promoted the peaceful uses of nuclear energy instead. This gave rise to the treaty's provisions that the nuclear weapons powers share their nuclear technology with the world's nonweapons states without reservation (Articles IV and V), that they work toward total disarmament (Article VI) but, that if nonweapons states felt threatened, they should be free to acquire nuclear weapons of their own (Article X).

Both the NPT's strategic concern with horizontal proliferation and its faith in finite deterrence are reflected in the treaty. To make sense of the NPT, however, one must choose which of these two premises should be controlling in interpreting the treaty's text and which is, in fact, sounder. All of this, in turn, requires an understanding of the NPT's history, which begins with the events that led to the first appeals for an NPT in 1958.

THE IRISH RESOLUTION AND THE FIRST NPT BARGAIN

In the late 1950s, experts who worried about nuclear proliferation were hardly concerned about the spread of nuclear materials and specialized equipment to such states as North Korea or Iran. Instead, they were focused on the actual and proposed U.S. transfer of nuclear weapons to Germany and members of the North Atlantic Treaty Organization (NATO) under what were called "dual key" control arrangements. Under this procedure, the Eisenhower administration began in the mid-1950s to deploy nuclear artillery in Europe for use by NATO forces. The United States retained custody of the nuclear artillery warheads, while U.S. and NATO armies were given nuclear-capable artillery tubes. If an occasion arose when the U.S. president decided that use of nuclear artillery was necessary, he could order the release of the nuclear warheads to the NATO commander, and the commander of the NATO ally where the artillery was deployed would give authority to release use of the nuclear-capable artillery tubes. Following this model, the United States deployed nuclear weapons not only to NATO ground forces, but U.S. and allied air forces in Europe while retaining control of the weapons.

Warsaw Pact members and the world's neutral powers, however, protested that U.S. authority over these weapons was less than complete. In 1956 and 1957, the Soviet Union objected to U.S. stationing of nuclear weapons in Germany and proposed a ban on the employment of nuclear weapons of any sort in Central Europe.[2] The United States, meanwhile, submitted a draft disarmament plan before the UN Disarmament Commission in which transfer of control of U.S. nuclear weapons to NATO allies was permitted if their use was necessary to fend off an armed attack.[3]

Concern with controls over such nuclear transfers was heightened further when in 1958 the U.S. Congress passed an amendment to the U.S. Atomic Energy Act that permitted the transfer of weapons materials, design information, and parts to nations that had "made substantial progress in the development of nuclear weapons."[4] Also, with the continued transfer of nuclear weapons to NATO, U.S. control arrangements became less rigid: One congressional investigation discovered German aircraft that were fueled, ready to take off at a moment's notice, and loaded with U.S. nuclear weapons.[5]

This trend toward more lax U.S. restraints on authority for the transfer of nuclear weapons came as progress toward disarmament negotiations in the UN had reached an impasse. The United States and the Soviet Union had agreed to a voluntary moratorium on nuclear testing in the fall of 1958, but the United States and its allies tied their continued adherence to this test ban to progress toward disarmament and a general easing of tensions. Last, but hardly least, the United States and the Soviet Union had threatened or considered using nuclear weapons on at least eight separate occasions since 1953.[6]

It was against this backdrop, then, that Irish Foreign Minister Frank Aiken offered a draft resolution concerning the "Further Dissemination of Nuclear Weapons" before the First Committee of the UN General Assembly on October 17, 1958. The resolution was quite modest, recognizing that "an increase in the number of states possessing nuclear weapons may occur, aggravating international tensions" and making disarmament "more difficult." It went on to recommend that the General Assembly establish an ad hoc committee to study the dangers inherent in the further dissemination of nuclear weapons.

Aiken offered to amend the resolution to urge parties to the UN's disarmament talks not to furnish nuclear weapons to any other nation while the negotiations were under way and to encourage other states to refrain from trying to manufacture nuclear weapons, but Western support for the amendment was thin. On October 31, 1958, Aiken withdrew the resolution when it became clear that no NATO nation was yet ready to endorse the initiative.[7]

The Irish, however, pursued the idea. The following year, Aiken resubmitted yet another version of the resolution to the General Assembly and made it clear that the proposal was a minimal proposition to which all parties ought agree. It was "hardly realistic," he argued, to expect any "early agreement on the abolition of nuclear weapons." "But what we can do," he argued, "is to reduce the risks which the spread of these weapons involves for this generation, and not to hand on to our children a problem even more difficult to solve than that with which we are now confronted." Indeed, Aiken argued, "if no such agreement is made, they [the nuclear powers] may well be forced by mutual fear and the pressure of their allies, to distribute these weapons, and so increase geometrically the danger of nuclear war."[8]

Why was such nuclear proliferation so dangerous and likely? Aiken gave two reasons. First, without an international nonproliferation agreement, "a sort of atomic *sauve-qui-peut*" was likely in which states "despairing of safety through collective action," would seek safety by getting nuclear weapons of their own. This trend was likely to get worse, since, in Aiken's view, there was "no conceivable addition" to the list of countries possessing nuclear weapons that would not undermine the pattern of regional and world politics that had "given the world the uneasy peace of the last few years."[9] Aiken made this same point even more graphically several years later:

The sudden appearance of nuclear weapons and their almost instantaneous long-range delivery systems in a previous nonnuclear state may be tantamount, in the circumstances of the world today, to pushing a gun through a neighbor's window . . . it may even be regarded as an act of war by neighboring countries who have not the second strike nuclear capacity possessed by great nuclear powers . . . (who) may be able to eliminate the threat by taking limited measures.[10]

Faced with such nuclear threats, nonweapons states, then, would try to acquire nuclear weapons from their nuclear armed allies, who, out of a misguided sense of political convenience, were likely to be cooperative. Yet, such cooperation, Aiken argued, would only give these smaller nations "the power to start a nuclear war, or to engage in nuclear blackmail, conceivably against a former ally." In short, without an international agreement against further nuclear weapons transfers, accidental and catalytic wars would become more likely and nations would drift into "a nightmare region in which man's powers of destruction are constantly increasing and his control over these powers is constantly diminishing."[11]

Aiken's second reason for believing the pace of proliferation would increase was the growing availability of civil nuclear reactor technology. As he explained before the UN, weapons-usable plutonium was a direct by-product of nuclear electrical power reactors, and these generators were now being built in nonweapons states. As such, it would become increasingly difficult for the governments of these countries to "resist domestic pressure to take the further step of producing nuclear weapons" on the "grounds of economy and security, if not for considerations of prestige."[12] Thus, the twin structures of Aiken's proposal: Weapons states should not furnish nuclear weapons to nonweapons states, and nonweapons states should refrain from trying to acquire them.

These views, although radical, were hardly unique. In fact, Aiken's arguments reflected the views of America's academic elite and were drawn in part from an American Academy of Arts and Sciences report on the problems of arms limitation. Subsequently published by the National Planning Association, this study, *The Nth Country Problem: A World Wide Survey of Nuclear Weapons Capabilities*, was previewed in *Daedalus* and *The Bulletin of the Atomic Scientists* and highlighted in a separate National Planning Report published in May 1958 entitled *1970 Without Arms Control*.[13]

This study's central contention was that "the problem of achieving international arms control will become vastly more difficult when the three powers having nuclear weapons are joined by a fourth, and then a fifth, and possibly more."[14] The reason why was the instability such proliferation threatened. As Aiken noted before the UN, quoting from The National Planning Report:

The possibility of accidental or of unauthorized use of atomic weapons will increase. Irresponsible "mischief-making" by one small nation could catalyze a nuclear conflict between larger powers, or might cause preexisting nonnuclear hostilities to escalate into nuclear hostilities.[15]

This instability, the report argued, was being aggravated by the nuclear superpowers' introduction of "quick reaction" ballistic missile delivery systems that "tend to be inflexible so that full-scale war may grow out of inadvertencies or deliberate mischief." These trends would make it "even more difficult to achieve and enforce arms control agreements, and much harder to inspire confidence in their effectiveness."[16] Whatever else nuclear weapons and nonweapons states might do to control the nuclear threat, then, it was clear it was in neither groups' interest to see nuclear weapons spread.[17] The study also emphasized that ultimately, progress against nuclear proliferation was only possible in the context of larger disarmament arrangements such as a comprehensive test ban and a military production cut-off backed by an effective international inspection system.[18]

These points together would shape an entire decade of NPT negotiations. Initially, however, Aiken chose only to emphasize the need to block the further horizontal proliferation of nuclear weapons to additional nations. In fact, at first he actually downplayed the dangers of continued superpower nuclear competition and denigrated demands to compensate nonweapons states for their pledged forbearance.

He conceded that nonweapons nations might consider it discriminatory to have to open up their nuclear activities to international inspections, while nuclear weapons nations did not. But this, Aiken insisted, was wrong thinking. In fact, nonweapons nations ought to welcome such inspections, since they might eventually serve as a test bed for regional arms control arrangements (e.g., European nuclear weapons free zones), which most nonweapons states already claimed they favored.[19]

As for making superpower nuclear disarmament a prerequisite for getting nonweapons states to back a nuclear nonproliferation treaty, Aiken believed this also was a mistake. The key reason for demanding a nonproliferation treaty, after all, was to address the proliferation threat without having to wait for the advent of nuclear disarmament. More important, the threat of nuclear war posed by the superpowers was pliable: Although "fraught with danger," Aiken argued, it was a threat "which we have managed to live with for a number of years" and for which "techniques" had been developed to deal with.[20] Instead of demanding nuclear disarmament first, the proper initial objective, then, was to get the superpowers to stop spreading nuclear weapons and to get nonweapons states to forswear acquiring them.

All of this should have reassured the United States and its allies. Initially, however, they had misgivings. As has already been noted, most NATO nations abstained when the Irish resolution was first put to a vote in 1958. In 1959, though, the Soviet Union also opposed the resolution, complaining that it was too permissive. As drafted, it would have allowed the United States to transfer nuclear weapons to European soil so long as the United States "retained control" of the weapons. France, meanwhile, abstained, arguing that the transfer of fissionable materials and nuclear weapons was difficult to control and that the real problem was ending manufacture of these items. At the time, France was developing its own nuclear arsenal and was assisting the Israelis in their nuclear weapons efforts as well.[21]

As for the United States, it actually decided to support the 1959 Irish resolution. Yet, when the resolution was modified in 1960 to call upon the weapons states to declare at once their intention to "refrain from relinquishing control of such weapons to any nation not possessing them and from transmitting to it the information necessary for their manufacture," the United States again objected. Although the Soviets decided to reverse themselves and supported the 1960 draft, the United States at the time was pushing the idea of giving NATO nuclear submarine missile boats of their own for a Multilateral Force (MLF). As such, the United States complained that the 1960 resolution failed to recognize the critical responsibility of the nuclear weapons nations. The U.S. representative went on to ask how the Irish could expect other nations to forgo nuclear weapons if the weapons states refused to end their own nuclear build-up. Besides, he argued, a commitment of indefinite duration of the sort the resolution called for was unverifiable.[22]

The United States again objected in 1961 when Sweden resubmitted a similar resolution, which recommended that

an inquiry be made into the conditions under which countries not possessing nuclear weapons might be willing to enter into specific undertakings to refrain from manufacturing or otherwise acquiring such weapons and to refuse to receive, in the future, nuclear weapons in their territories on behalf of any other country.[23]

The resolution's new language gave the United States cause for concern. Now the resolution was no longer focused on restraining weapons nations from "relinquishing control" of nuclear weapons, but on getting nonweapons nations to refuse receiving nuclear weapons in their territories; that is, all of NATO was being asked to stop hosting U.S. nuclear weapons. This was hardly lost on the Soviets, who immediately incorporated the Swedish language (i.e., "refrain from transferring control" and "refuse to admit the nuclear weapons of any other states into their territories") into their own draft treaty for general and complete disarmament in 1962.[24]

Not surprisingly, the United States objected to the Swedish resolution, complaining that it effectively called "into question the right of free nations to join together in collective self-defense, including the right of self-defense with nuclear weapons if need be." Yet, the United States representative at the UN was equally at pains to emphasize that the United States supported the goal of nonproliferation. His proof: The U.S. Draft Program for General and Complete Disarmament, like the Irish Resolution, required nuclear weapons states to "refrain from relinquishing *control*" of nuclear weapons to nonweapons states.[25]

For the next four years, the United States continued to insist that it was interested in promoting nuclear nonproliferation.[26] However, it opposed a variety of nonproliferation resolutions backed by the Soviets, Swedes, and others, which, if accepted, would jeopardize existing nuclear sharing arrangements with NATO or the possibility of creating a multilateral nuclear force for a "United States of Europe." Ultimately, the United States only became focused on reaching an international nuclear nonproliferation agreement when it became clear that Germany and other NATO nations were not keen on reaching an MLF agreement. With this proposal disposed of and the Soviets willing to accept language that would allow the United States to deploy nuclear weapons to NATO (assuming they were kept under U.S. control), the United States was ready to negotiate a nonproliferation agreement.[27]

FINITE DETERRENCE AND NUCLEAR "RIGHTS"

By early 1966, however, the terms of UN debate over proliferation had changed. In 1958, the horizontal spread of nuclear weapons (and the accidental or catalytic wars it might prompt) were seen as the primary threat to world security. At the same time, deterrence between the nuclear superpowers was viewed, as Aiken argued, as being relatively stable. By the early 1960s, the reverse became the common view among arms experts. Now it was the nuclear weapons states' continued efforts to refine and expand their arsenals that was considered to be most likely to precipitate unintended nuclear wars. As India's UN representative put it in 1966:

[The] dangers of dissemination and independent manufacture [of nuclear weapons] pale into the background when one views the calamitous dangers of the arms race which is developing today as a result of the proliferation of nuclear weapons by the nuclear weapon Powers themselves, large and small. For many years now, the Super-Powers have possessed an over-kill or multiple-destruction capacity and even their second-strike capabilities are sufficient to destroy the entire world. They have hundreds of missiles of varying ranges which are capable of devastating the surface of the earth. They are continuing to test underground, miniaturizing warheads, improving penetration capabilities and sophisticating their weapons and missiles. The other nuclear weapons powers are also following the same menacing path, conducting atmospheric weapons tests, proceeding from manned-bomber delivery systems to missile systems and submarines. . . . It is here that the proliferation of nuclear weapons has its most catastrophic consequences.[28]

Why this shift in thinking? Beginning in the late 1950s, a new theory of nuclear stability, known as finite deterrence, emerged in academic and military writings. According to this view, smaller nations could keep larger nuclear powers from threatening them militarily by acquiring a small number of nuclear weapons of their own. With their limited nuclear arsenal, the smaller nations might not be able to prevail in war against a larger power but could effectively "tear an arm off," by targeting the larger nation's key cities and, thus, deter such nations from attacking them. A corollary to this point was a critique of the constant quantitative and qualitative improvement of the superpowers' strategic offensive and defensive forces. This build-up was considered to be unnecessary and provocative. Because a nation only needed a small nuclear arsenal to threaten to destroy an opponent's major cities, anything more, it was argued, was wasteful and only likely to encourage ever greater nuclear arms preparations between rivals. The greatest nuclear danger, finite deterrence proponents insisted, was not accidental or catalytic wars that the horizontal spread of nuclear weapons might prompt, but rather the unintended wars that continued "vertical" proliferation of the superpowers' arsenals might ignite. As the superpowers increased the size of their nuclear weapons stockpiles and reduced the amount of time needed to deliver them precisely on target, these experts argued that the possibility of accidental nuclear wars occurring through miscalculation steadily increased.[29]

The earliest manifestations of this view in NPT negotiations came as smaller states tired of the superpowers' unwillingness to move on any agreement until the NATO nuclear sharing issue was resolved. As has been noted, in 1961 the Swedes submitted a resolution before the UN General Assembly calling for an inquiry as to the conditions under which nonweapons states might be willing to "refrain from acquiring nuclear weapons." The idea here was to force the nuclear weapons states to support reaching an agreement on nonproliferation by demonstrating the popularity of concluding such a treaty and by threatening to proceed without them. The very premise of the Swedish inquiry—that nonweapons nations would acquire nuclear weapons unless certain "conditions" were met—however, was clearly at odds with Aiken's original arguments that nonproliferation was equally a security imperative for both weapons and nonweapons states. Indeed, it suggested that smaller states' acquisition of nuclear weapons was reasonable *unless* they received something in exchange for not proceeding.

This thinking was reflected in the 1962 replies to the UN secretary-general's inquiry concerning the conditions under which nonweapons states might refrain from acquiring nuclear weapons. Of the sixty-two nations that replied, most wanted specific neighbors or all the states within their region to forswear acquiring nuclear weapons as a condition for them doing likewise. But several nations, including Italy, wanted nothing less than a halt in the superpowers' nuclear build-up.[30] This view received additional support from the three Western nuclear powers (the United States, Great Britain, and France) that answered the inquiry. For them, as well, general and complete disarmament was the best solution.[31]

For the next two years, debate over the merits of establishing a European MLF made it nearly impossible for the Soviets, the United States, and most NATO nations to reach any agreement over any nuclear issue.[32] In an effort to square the desire for disarmament and the need for some immediate action on proliferation, India and Sweden (both of whom were considering acquiring nuclear weapons of their own)[33] suggested a new approach in June 1965. What they recommended to the UN Disarmament Commission was a nonproliferation agreement combined with measures that would begin to cap the arms race between the superpowers. Italy also suggested that there be a time limit on how long nonnuclear nations had to refrain from acquiring nuclear weapons. This limit—a kind of nuclear coercive leverage in potentia—it was argued, would serve as an "inducement" to the superpowers to disarm. With support from the world's nonaligned nations, the resolution passed overwhelmingly.[34]

From this point on, the debate over reaching a nuclear nonproliferation agreement *presumed* that nonweapons nations had a right to acquire nuclear weapons and that the only question was what they should get in exchange for not exercising it. Each nation protected their right in a different fashion. For the Chinese, it was essential for the non-nuclear nations not to be "deprived of their freedom to develop nuclear weapons to resist U.S.-Soviet nuclear threats."[35] For Egypt, it was a sovereign prerogative only to be renounced if the superpowers made clear how they intended to disarm. As Egypt's representative to the UN disarmament talks explained:

The nonnuclear countries will in law renounce their right to nuclear weapons, but nuclear stockpiles and the threat of a nuclear confrontation will in fact continue to exist indefinitely. . . . This de facto situation could always constitute an incitement to manufacture or acquire nuclear weapons. To diminish this risk still further it will be necessary, pending the complete elimination by radical measures of nuclear stockpiles and the nuclear threat, to include in the treaty a formal and definite indication of what the nuclear Powers propose to do with the existing nuclear armaments.[36]

For Brazil, however, the prerogative to go nuclear entailed nothing less than their right to self-defense. As Brazil's representative explained:

If a country renounces the procurement or production by its own national means of effective deterrents against nuclear attack or the threat thereof, it must be assured that renunciation—a step taken because of higher considerations of the interests of mankind—will not entail irreparable danger to its own people. The public could never be made to understand why a government, in forswearing its defense capability, had not at the same time provided reasonable and lasting assurances that the nation would not be directly or indirectly, the object of total destruction or of nuclear blackmail.

For the Brazilians, this meant that any nuclear nonproliferation agreement had to include guarantees that nuclear weapons states would not use or threaten to use their weapons against nonweapons states.[37]

Other states, however, thought that nuclear disarmament was necessary. Tunisia, like Brazil, was "not happy about renouncing their right to acquire nuclear weapons," but thought that it was too poor of a nation ever to try to acquire them and, thus, could only be truly secure in a disarmed world. Sweden, which was still developing a nuclear weapons option of its own, shared Tunisia's views but saw giving up "the most powerful weaponry that has ever been produced by man" as something it, as one of the "smaller and more defenseless nations," could only do if the superpowers disarmed.[38]

Once it was established that nonweapons nations had a sovereign right to acquire nuclear weapons and that they should be compensated in some fashion for renouncing their intention to exercise it, it was only a short step further to suggest that they should be allowed to develop sensitive nuclear technology so they would not be deprived of nuclear energy's "peaceful" benefits. India, whose president had just decided to develop a "peaceful" nuclear explosive option, was the most outspoken in the UN in defending its "right" to "unrestricted" development of nuclear energy. This, in part, reflected India's well-known opposition to international safeguards, which it had objected to since the early 1950s because they would interfere in India's development and its "inalienable right" to "produce and hold the fissionable material required for [India's] peaceful power programs." After China exploded its first nuclear device in May 1964, India's desire to protect this right became even more imperative. As the Indian external affairs minister explained in 1967:

Most of the countries represented at the disarmament committee appreciated India's peculiar position with regard to the nonproliferation treaty. . . . China would be a nuclear state which would not be called upon to undertake any obligations. India could have become a nuclear country if it had exploded the bomb as China did. But because India had shown restraint, a desire for peace, and opposition to the spread of nuclear armaments, under this treaty it would find itself in a much worse position than China. . . . The result of our restraint is that we are a nonnuclear power which will have to suffer all the disadvantages. On the other hand, China, which has shown no restraint, will not suffer from any disadvantage even if it signs the treaty, as it is already a nuclear power.[39]

What were the Indians talking about? The external affairs minister left little doubt: every nuclear "advantage" the weapons nations enjoyed, including nuclear testing. After all, the draft nonproliferation treaty would "seriously hamper and impede" peaceful nuclear research, since it would prevent nonnuclear countries from undertaking underground explosions for the purpose of carrying out nuclear research while imposing no such obligation on nuclear weapons states. The ability to produce weapons-usable materials free from intrusive and discriminatory

international safeguards and the freedom to develop all aspects of nuclear energy including "peaceful" nuclear explosives, he argued, was
critical to secure India's "sovereign right of unrestricted development"
of nuclear energy.[40]

If it were just India that was making these arguments, they might be
dismissed as being peculiar to a nation claiming it was "exposed to nuclear blackmail" and who, incidentally, was working on a "civilian" nuclear explosive program. Yet, in making its case, India was able to cite
the views of Brazil's representative who argued that

nuclear energy plays a decisive role in [the] mobilization of resources. We must
develop and utilize it in every form, including the explosives that make possible
not only great civil engineering projects but also an ever-increasing variety of
applications that may prove essential to speed up the progress of our peoples.
To accept the self-limitation requested from us in order to secure the monopoly
of the present nuclear-weapon Powers would amount to renouncing in advance
boundless prospects in the field of peaceful activities.[41]

Of course, Brazil was also developing a nuclear weapons option at the
time.[42] It would be wrong, however, to view Brazil and India's interest
in peaceful nuclear explosives (PNEs) without reference to the United
States. America, after all, had been touting the possible advantages of
peaceful nuclear explosives since the early 1960s in arguing against
reaching a comprehensive nuclear test ban with the Soviets. The United
States also was enthusiastic about the need to develop fast breeder reactors that would use reprocessed plutonium fuels.[43] Thus, Nigeria, Mexico, and Ethiopia, who had no nuclear power programs of any sort, were
every bit as insistent as India and Brazil that any treaty on nonproliferation not place them "in a position of perpetual inferiority in any field
of knowledge."[44] Nigeria's recommendation to solve this problem was

that non-nuclear weapons powers would not only have nuclear explosives,
through an international organization, for their peaceful projects but also have
opportunities for their scientists to develop to the fullest their intellectual capabilities in all fields, including that of nuclear-explosive technology.[45]

These nations were just as insistent that whatever international safeguards the NPT required not interfere with their development of new
power reactors and fuels. In this they were joined by Japan and Germany, who feared that the United States and Soviet Union would use
the NPT's safeguard provisions to steal industrial nuclear secrets from
their civil nuclear programs. As Germany's foreign minister explained
in 1967:

The unhindered civilian utilization of the atom is a vital interest of the Federal Republic. . . . It is known that German scientists are working with the prospect of success on the development of the second generation of reactors, the so-called fast breeders. . . . We go on the assumption that the placing into effect of controls does not interfere with the economic operations of factories, does not lead to the loss of production secrets, but counters the dangers of misuse. For this purpose it is adequate to control the end-product points, and to have a control which possibly could be exercised by automated instruments.[46]

Germany's foreign minister added that nations like his own were already apprehensive of the nuclear weapons states trying to monopolize the civilian nuclear field by dint of their commanding lead in military nuclear technology. At least as great a worry, he argued, was the extent to which inspections under the proposed NPT might compromise the pace and secrecy of nonweapons states' civil nuclear development.[47]

In the end, the NPT's preamble and Article III stipulated that nations, such as Germany, could meet their safeguards obligations through somewhat less threatening but "equivalent" procedures under EURATOM, that inspections would be restricted to monitoring the flows of source and fissionable materials at "certain strategic points," and that they would be designed "to avoid hampering the economic or technological development of the Parties."

The NPT also emphasized in Articles IV and V that nothing in the treaty should be "interpreted as affecting the inalienable right of all the Parties to the Treaty to develop research, production and use of nuclear energy for peaceful purposes without discrimination." Indeed, the treaty called on all parties to "undertake to facilitate" the "fullest possible exchange of equipment, materials, and technological information for the peaceful uses of nuclear energy." The treaty established procedures for sharing the benefits of peaceful nuclear explosives, although it prohibited the direct transfer of explosive devices to or the development of such devices by nonweapons states.

Finally, the treaty called on the weapons states in Article VI "to pursue negotiations in good faith on effective measures relating to the cessation of the nuclear arms race at an early date and to nuclear disarmament." Even the Italians' suggestion to leverage the superpower nuclear reductions—that six months before the end of a fixed duration, nations could give notice of their intent to withdraw from the treaty—was retained after a fashion in Article X. The Italians' specific six-month option was rejected along with Nigerian demands that the NPT explicitly empower members to withdraw if the treaty's disarmament aims were "being frustrated."[48] But it was agreed that the treaty would not be of indefinite duration. Instead, it would last twenty-five years and be reviewed as to whether or not it should be extended and, if so, how. As the Swiss noted, it was "preferable" that the treaty be "concluded for a definite period" so as to avoid "tying" the hands of nonweapons states who could not be expected to wait indefinitely on the weapons states to disarm.[49] Also, it was agreed that any party to the treaty, under Article X, retained the right to withdraw with three month's notice if it "decides that extraordinary events, related to the subject matter of this treaty, have jeopardized the supreme interests of its country."[50]

WHAT BARGAIN WAS STRUCK?

Reading the NPT today, much of this history is still relevant. Certainly, the original bargain of the Irish resolutions of the late 1950s is clearly reflected in the treaty's first two articles, which prohibit the direct or indirect transfer and receipt of nuclear weapons, nuclear explosives, or control over such devices. The Irish resolutions are also reflected in Article III, which calls on all treaty parties to accept and negotiate a system of safeguards that would "[prevent] diversion of nuclear energy from peaceful uses to nuclear weapons or other nuclear explosive devices." Finally, the treaty makes it clear in Article IV that parties to the NPT could only exercise their right to develop peaceful nuclear energy "in conformity with articles I and II."

Beyond this, the NPT's framers made it clear that they shared Foreign Minister Aiken's original concerns about horizontal proliferation. The Germans, for example, defended the NPT "because it is frightening to think what would happen if possession of nuclear weapons were spread chaotically through the world, if some adventurous state were one day irresponsibly to use such a weapon." Echoing this view, Germany's foreign minister argued that "even only one additional nuclear power would start a chain reaction that would be hard to control."[51] The Canadians made essentially the same point, arguing that some discrimination against nonweapons states was "the only alternative to allowing the continued spread of nuclear weapons . . . and such a process in the end would have no other result than nuclear war . . . on the greatest scale."[52] The British representative to the General Assembly was just as emphatic:

We are concerned not only that new possessors of nuclear weapons may employ them against each other, or against a non-nuclear state; we see an even greater danger in the possibility that the use of nuclear weapons by a third country could precipitate a war which would end in a nuclear exchange between the two so-called Superpowers. In our view, and I would think in that of the Soviet Union as well, each additional nuclear power increases the possibility of nuclear war, by design, by miscalculation, or even by accident.[53]

On the other hand, there were more than a few UN representatives who viewed the NPT and its key provisions through the lens of finite deterrence. By this light, horizontal proliferation threats were simply derivative of the superpowers' arms race and of less import. As India's UN representative explained:

Further proliferation is only the consequence of past and present proliferation and unless we halt the actual and current proliferation of nuclear weapons [in nuclear weapons states], it will not be possible to deal effectively with the problematic danger of further proliferation among additional countries.[54]

Clearly, this view, along with the idea that all states had inalienable rights to unhindered access to civilian nuclear technology and to withdraw from the NPT if the superpowers did not disarm or if their security interests were at serious risk, were behind Articles IV, V, VI, and X as well as most of the NPT's preamble. The wording of Articles I and II, in contrast, had remained virtually unchanged since the beginning of negotiations in the early 1960s and reflected the original Irish concerns about the accidental and catalytic nuclear wars that further horizontal proliferation might prompt.

Unfortunately, the two views are at odds. Certainly, it is difficult to argue that the further spread of even small numbers of nuclear weapons to other nations will significantly increase the risk of accidental or catalytic nuclear war and, yet, at the same time, assume that nonweapons states have a residual right to acquire such weapons to get the world's weapons states to limit their own nuclear arsenals. Thus, the debate over what constituted "peaceful" nuclear development "in conformity with articles I and II" under Article IV and what effective safeguards "with a view to preventing diversion" under Article III might require.

Those who believed that the superpowers' arms build-up was the key threat to peace, insisted upon allowing the world's nonnuclear states unhindered access to nuclear energy technology if it was not intended for bombs. In their view, it would be unfair to deprive the world's nuclear have nots of this technology (which the world's nuclear weapons states were already enjoying) after securing their avowal not to acquire nuclear weapons. As they saw it, so long as nuclear transfers were made under established safeguards procedures, they automatically should be viewed as being "in conformity with Articles I and II." Thus, the Dutch, Belgians, and Luxembourgeois and, at times, even the Americans saw the line between safeguarded and unsafeguarded activities under the NPT as being quite bright.[55] As the Dutch representative explained, unless it was clear that the nuclear assistance was going to build nuclear weapons, it should be assumed it was not:

My delegation interprets Article I of the draft treaty to mean that assistance by supplying knowledge, materials and equipment cannot be denied to a non-nuclear-weapon State until it is clearly established that such assistance will be used for the manufacture of nuclear weapons or other nuclear devices. In other words, in all cases where the recipient parties to the treaty have conformed with the provisions of Article III, there should be a clear presumption that the assistance rendered will not be used for the manufacture of nuclear weapons and other explosive devices.[56]

The Americans were just as insistent that "peaceful applications of energy derived from controlled and sustained nuclear reactions—that is, reactions stopping far short of explosion" had "nothing to do with nuclear weapons" and, thus, development of such applications would not be affected by the NPT's prohibitions.[57] As the U.S. State Department's own Policy Planning Staff explained in an internal study:

After the NPT, many nations can be expected to take advantage of the terms of the treaty to produce quantities of fissionable material. Plutonium separation plants will be built; fast breeder reactors developed. It is possible that experimentation with conventional explosives that might be relevant to detonating a nuclear bomb core may take place. In this way, various nations will attain a well developed option on a bomb. A number of nations will be able to detonate a bomb within a year following withdrawal from the treaty; others may even shorten this period.[58]

Most NPT negotiators, however, felt uncomfortable with so presumptive a view. Thus, Spanish and Mexican attempts to create a duty on the part of the nuclear haves to provide nuclear energy aid to the nuclear have nots and to reference "the entire technology of reactors and fuels" in the NPT's text were explicitly rejected.[59] According to some analysts, this rejection suggested that the NPT's framers understood that some forms of civil nuclear energy—for example, weapons-usable nuclear fuels and their related production facilities—were so close to bomb making that sharing them might not be in "conformity" with Articles I and II. The NPT's framers, they argue, understood that inspections that lived up to Article III's requirement to "avoid hampering" nations' "technological development," and that were in accordance with the NPT's desire to focus on the "flow" of source and special fissionable materials at "certain strategic points" would have difficulty accounting for significant quantities of weapons-usable materials at enrichment and reprocessing facilities or at reactors that used weapons-usable fuels and at their respective fuel fabrication plants. Nor in these cases would timely warning of diversions be likely. As such, mere inspections of such materials and activities would only mask the probable transfer or acquisition of nuclear weapons. This, in turn, would violate the NPT's prohibitions in Articles

I and II and Article III's stricture that safeguards serve the purpose of verifying member nations' fulfillment of their NPT obligations.[60]

Unfortunately, the NPT's negotiating record alone can hardly clarify these matters. Indeed, tensions between the first three articles and those that follow in the NPT still exist today. Unaligned nations such as Indonesia and Mexico still argue that weapons states must go much further in reducing their nuclear arsenals and in sharing the benefits of peaceful nuclear energy to keep nonweapons states from abandoning the NPT. And the issue of just what constitutes effective safeguards under the treaty for trouble nations such as North Korea, Libya, Iran, Algeria, and Iraq and for dangerous nuclear activities such as reprocessing in Japan, is as much a concern as ever.

It is worth noting, however, that a number of things have changed since 1968. Instead of a bipolar rivalry that had existed during the cold war, today there is only one superpower—the United States. Rather than an ever-escalating nuclear arms race, the United States and former Soviet republics, moreover, are now cooperating in nuclear weapons reductions. Nor is the supposed stability that might come from threatening to attack an opponent's cities anywhere near as sound as once supposed. Indeed, with the release and analysis of information on the cold war, it now appears that nuclear deterrence even between the superpowers was anything but automatic or guaranteed.[61] As for finite deterrence, it has proved to be neither as cheap nor easy as originally promised. In the case of the French, the original innovators of this theory, developing and maintaining a French finite deterrence force (the Force de Frappe) has required annually spending billions of dollars to field several generations of strategic systems that have never seemed quite credible (or survivable enough) even against a limited Soviet attack. Smaller nations, such as India and Pakistan, now aiming to deter their near nuclear neighbors or existing weapons states, are likely to face similar challenges that proportionately will be at least as stressful.[62]

As for the promised benefits of peaceful nuclear power, these too now seem less compelling. Certainly, few, if any nations, now believe peaceful nuclear explosives promise any economic benefits. The United States, India, and Russia—the only nations to experiment with such devices— no longer use them, and even Brazil and Argentina, who initially rejected the NPT because it would not allow them to acquire such devices, have renounced their development. Economically viable nuclear electricity, meanwhile, has been limited to uranium-fueled thermal reactors operating only in the largest economies in North America, Europe, and East Asia. The economical use of weapons-usable plutonium or mixed-oxide fuels in thermal or fast reactors is, at best, still many decades away.[63]

Meanwhile, the security dangers of nuclear power in certain regions have become all too apparent. Iraq, Iran, North Korea, and Algeria all have nuclear energy programs that are monitored by the IAEA. Yet, all harbor a desire to develop nuclear weapons and have attempted to evade IAEA inspections. It is unclear if even special IAEA inspections could provide sufficient warning of dangerous activities in these politically turbulent nations.[64] IAEA monitoring of plutonium fabrication and reprocessing activities in such stable nations as Japan have also been criticized as being dangerously deficient. In fact, the amount of weapons-usable materials such plants are producing threatens to exceed the amount of fissile material currently present in weapon state arsenals.[65]

This brings us to the first indications of the NPT's limitations. These emerged shortly after efforts were begun to determine precisely what should be safeguarded under the treaty and how, a task assumed by the Zangger Committee (named after its chairman, Claude Zangger of Switzerland), which first met in 1971.[66] This committee developed a trigger list of items and nuclear materials that should be subject to IAEA safeguards, but the key nuclear supplier nations did not adopt it until they were compelled to do so by an event that the NPT's framers hoped would never happen. In May 1974, India exploded a "peaceful" nuclear device that employed "civilian" U.S., Canadian, and Western European reprocessing and heavy water technology and hardware. Although India had not signed the NPT, this event, perhaps more than any other, raised doubts about the adequacy of merely securing peaceful end-use pledges in exchange for supplying sensitive civilian nuclear technology—an approach many NPT proponents had hoped would be sufficient.[67] Worse still, for those states demanding nuclear equality, it soon gave rise to international control efforts that were explicitly discriminatory.

NOTES

1. See, for example, Lawrence Scheinman, *The International Atomic Energy Agency and World Nuclear Order* (Washington, D.C.: Resources for the Future, 1987), 18; Ian Smart, "A Defective Dream," 79; Bertrand Goldschmidt, "From Nuclear Middle Ages to Nuclear Renaissance," 111; Sigvard Eklund, "Reliable Supply: Respecting the 'Rules of the Game,' " 164; and Donald M. Kerr, "Future Unlike the Past," 213, all contained in *Atoms for Peace: An Analysis after Thirty Years*, edited by Joseph F. Pilat (Boulder, CO: Westview Press, 1985).

2. See "Soviet Proposal Introduced in the Disarmament Subcommittee: Reduction of Armaments and Armed Forces and the Prohibition of Atomic and Hydrogen Weapons, May 18, 1957," in U.S. Department of State, *Documents on Disarmament, 1945–1959* (Washington, D.C.: USGPO, 1960) Vol. 2, 756–57.

3. See "Western Working Paper Submitted to the Disarmament Subcommittee: Proposals for Partial Measures of Disarmament, August 29, 1957," in U.S. Department of State, *Documents on Disarmament, 1945–1959*, Vol. 2, 879.

4. The Atomic Energy Act of 1954, U.S. Code secs. 54, 64, 82, 91(c), 92 as amended (1954).

5. See George Bunn, *Arms Control by Committee: Managing Negotiations with the Russians* (Stanford, CA: Stanford University Press, 1992), 62.

6. The Eisenhower administration had threatened to use or consider using nuclear weapons to end the Korean War in 1953, to save the French in Vietnam in 1954, to save the Republic of China in 1954, 1955, and 1958, and to prevent any invasion of Kuwait in 1958. Atomic howitzers also were deployed by U.S. forces landing in Lebanon in 1958, and Russia threatened the use of nuclear weapons to end the Suez crisis in 1956. See Peter Lyon, *Eisenhower: Portrait of the Hero* (Boston: Little, Brown and Company, 1974), 534, 541, 583, 606, 610, 624, 639–40, 719, 775–76, 784.

7. The resolution initially passed with thirty-seven affirmative votes, but forty-four nations—including the United States, the United Kingdom, Italy, Japan, France, Greece, Belgium, Turkey, and the Netherlands—abstained. See "Irish Draft Resolution Introduced in the First Committee of the General Assembly: Further Dissemination of Nuclear Weapons, October 17, 1958," in U.S. Department of State, *Documents on Disarmament, 1945–1959*, vol. 2, 1185–86.

8. See "Statement by Irish Foreign Minister (Aiken) to the First Committee of the General Assembly, September 23 and November 13, 1959," in U.S. Department of State, *Documents on Disarmament 1945–1959*, vol. 2, 1474–78, 1520–26.

9. Ibid.

10. See "Statement of Irish Foreign Minister (Aiken) to the First Committee of the General Assembly, November 6, 1962," in U.S. Arms Control and Disarmament Agency, *Documents on Disarmament 1962* (Washington, D.C.: USGPO, 1963), 1025–28.

11. See "Statement by the Irish Foreign Minister, November 13, 1959," in U.S. Department of State, *Documents on Disarmament 1945–1959*, vol. 2, 1520–26. In this speech, Foreign Minister Aiken attributes these views to Howard Simons, cited in note 13.

12. Ibid.

13. See David Inglis, "The Fourth Country Problem: Let's Stop at Three," *Bulletin of the Atomic Scientists* (January 1959): 22–26; Howard Simons, "World-Wide Capabilities for Production and Control of Nuclear Weapons," *Daedalus* 88, no. 3 (Summer 1959): 385–409; William C. Davidson, Marvin I. Kalkstein, and Christophe Hohenemser, *The Nth Country Problem and Arms Control* (Washington D.C.: National Planning Association, January 1960), 108; and National Planning Association, *1970 Without Arms Control* (Washington, D.C.: National Planning Association, May 1958), 104.

14. National Planning Assoc., *1970 Without Arms Control*, 10.

15. Davidson, et al., *The Nth Country Problem and Arms Control*, xi.

16. Ibid.

17. See, for example, the conclusion in Simons, "World-Wide Capabilities," 407.

18. See the findings in Davidson, et al., *The Nth Country Problem and Arms Control*, xix.

19. See "Statement by the Irish Foreign Minister, November 13, 1959," in U.S. Department of State, *Documents on Disarmament 1945–1959*, vol. 2, 1520–26; and "Statement of Irish Foreign Minister, November 6, 1962," in U.S. Arms Control, *Documents on Disarmament 1962*, 1025–28.

20. See "Statement by the Irish Foreign Minister, November 13, 1959," in U.S. Department of State, *Documents on Disarmament 1945–1959*, vol. 2, 1520–26.

21. See Lawrence Scheinman, *Atomic Energy Policy in France under the Fourth Republic* (Princeton, NJ: Princeton University Press, 1965), 183 ff.; and Avner Cohen, "Stumbling into Opacity: The United States, Israel, and the Atom, 1960–63," *Security Studies* 4, no. 2 (Winter 1994): 199–200; and *Israel and the Bomb* (New York: Columbia University Press, 1998), 57–60, 73–75.

22. See United Nations Department of Political and Security Council Affairs, *The United Nations and Disarmament 1945–1970* (New York: United Nations Publications, 1971), 260–61.

23. The Swedish submitted this resolution, 1664 (XVI), December 4, 1961. See ibid., 265.

24. Ibid.

25. See "Statement by the United States Representative (Yost) to the First Committee of the General Assembly: Spread of Nuclear Weapons, November 30, 1961," in U.S. Arms Control and Disarmament Agency, *Documents on Disarmament, 1961* (Washington, D.C.: USGPO, 1962), 691–92.

26. See, for example, "Statement by ACDA Director Foster to the Eighteen Nation Disarmament Committee: Nondissemination of Nuclear Weapons, February 6, 1964," in U.S. Arms Control and Disarmament Agency, *Documents on Disarmament, 1964* (Washington, D.C.: USGPO, 1965), 32–33. Here, U.S. officials made the case for international nuclear nonproliferation restraint, since without it there "would be no rest for anyone . . . no stability, no real security and no chance of effective disarmament" and because the acquisition of nuclear weapons by smaller countries would "increase the likelihood of the great Powers becoming involved in what would otherwise remain local conflicts."

27. See Bunn, *Arms Control by Committee*, 66–75.

28. See "Statement by the Indian Representative (Trivedi) to the First Committee of the General Assembly: Nonproliferation of Nuclear Weapons, October 31, 1966," in U.S. Arms Control and Disarmament Agency, *Documents on Disarmament, 1966* (Washington, D.C.: USGPO, 1967), 679.

29. For the earliest popular presentations of finite deterrence theory see Pierre M. Gallois, "Nuclear Aggression and National Suicide," *The Reporter*, November 18, 1958, 23–26; P. H. Backus, "Finite Deterrence, Controlled Retaliation," *U.S. Naval Institute Proceedings* (March 1959): 23–29; and George W. Rathjens, Jr. "Deterrence and Defense," *Bulletin of the Atomic Scientists* (September 1958): 225–28. Elements of this line of thinking, especially with regard to the desirability of capping the superpowers' arms build-up could also be found in the American studies cited in note 13 that Aiken selectively quoted from when he first submitted his UN nonproliferation resolutions in 1958 and 1959.

30. In fact, Italy first voiced reservations about agreeing not to acquire nuclear weapons unless the nuclear weapons nations promised to disarm in a NATO gathering held in February 1962. Later that year, however, it acquiesced and supported a U.S. draft resolution that would allow the use of U.S. weapons by a multilateral NATO naval force. For details see George Bunn, Roland M. Timerbaev, and James F. Leonard, "Nuclear Disarmament: How Much Have the Five Nuclear Powers Promised in the Non-Proliferation Treaty," in *At the Nuclear*

Crossroads, edited by John B. Rhinelander and Adam M. Scheinman (Lanham, MD: University Press of America, 1995), 15.

31. See United Nations, *Disarmament 1945–1970*, 266.

32. See, for example, the exchange between the Soviet and U.S. representatives to the Eighteen-Nation Disarmament Committee July 2, 1964, in U.S. Arms Control, *Documents on Disarmament, 1964*, 241–56.

33. On Sweden's nuclear weapons efforts at the time and India's debate and decision in 1965 to develop "peaceful" nuclear explosives, see Steve Coll, "Neutral Sweden Quietly Keeps Nuclear Option Open," *The Washington Post*, November 25, 1964, A1; and George Perkovich, *India's Nuclear Bomb* (Berkeley: University of California Press, 1999), 60–85.

34. The resolution is discussed in United Nations, *Disarmament 1945–1970*, 269. Italy and others continued for the next two years to promote the idea of freeing nations of their nonproliferation obligations if the superpowers failed to disarm. See, for example, "Statement by the Burmese Representative (Maung Maung) to the Eighteen-Nation Disarmament Committee: Nonproliferation of Nuclear Weapons, October 10, 1967" and "Statement by the Italian Representative (Caracciolo) to the Eighteen-Nation Disarmament Committee: Draft Nonproliferation Treaty, October 24, 1967," in U.S. Arms Control and Disarmament Agency, *Documents on Disarmament, 1967* (Washington, D.C.: USGPO, 1968), 463, 529.

35. See, for example, "Chinese Communist Comment on Draft Nonproliferation Treaty, September 3, 1967," in U.S. Arms Control, *Documents on Disarmament, 1967*, 381.

36. See "Statement of the Egyptian Representative (Khallaf) to the Eighteen-Nation Committee on Disarmament, March 3, 1966," U.S. Arms Control, *Documents on Disarmament, 1966*, 156–57.

37. See "Statement by the Brazilian Representative (Azeredo da Silveira) to the Eighteen-Nation Disarmament Committee: Draft Nonproliferation Treaty, August 31, 1967," in U.S. Arms Control, *Documents on Disarmament, 1967*, 370.

38. See "Address by President Bourguiba of Tunisia to the General Assembly {Extract}, September 27, 1967," and "Statement by the Swedish Representative (Myrdal) to the Eighteen-Nation Disarmament Committee: Nonproliferation of Nuclear Weapons, October 3, 1967," in U.S. Arms Control, *Documents on Disarmament, 1967*, 429, 444.

39. See "Extract from News Conference Remarks by the Indian External Affairs Minister (Chagla), April 27, 1967," in U.S. Arms Control, *Documents on Disarmament, 1967*, 204–5.

40. Ibid.

41. See ibid., and "Statement by the Brazilian Representative (Correa da Costa) to the Eighteen-Nation Disarmament Committee: Peaceful Uses of Nuclear Energy, May 18, 1967," in U.S. Arms Control, *Documents on Disarmament, 1967*, 226.

42. For a brief description of Brazil's attempt to secure an unsafeguarded military production reactor during this period see Leonard S. Spector, *Nuclear Proliferation Today* (New York: Vintage Books, 1984), 236–38.

43. See Albert Wohlstetter et al., *Swords from Plowshares: The Military Potential of Civilian Nuclear Energy*, (Chicago: University of Chicago Press, 1979), 85–86, and Wohlstetter, et al., "The Spread of Nuclear Bombs: Predictions, Premises, Policies," vol. I-1 of *Can We Make Nuclear Power Compatible with Limiting the Spread*

of Nuclear Weapons? (Los Angeles: Pan Heuristics, November 15, 1976, ERDA Contract E(49–1)-3747), 9–32, 89–108.

44. See, for example "Statement by the Ethiopian Representative (Zelleke) to the Eighteen-Nation Disarmament Committee: Nonproliferation of Nuclear Weapons, October 5, 1967"; and "Statement by the Mexican Representative (Castaneda) to the Eighteen-Nation Disarmament Committee: Latin American Nuclear-Free Zone, May 18, 1967," in U.S. Arms Control, *Documents on Disarmament, 1967,* 228, 449–50.

45. See "Statement by the Nigerian Representative (Sule Kolo) to the Eighteen-Nation Disarmament Committee: Draft Nonproliferation Treaty, August 31, 1967," in U.S. Arms Control, *Documents on Disarmament, 1967,* 377. The Germans also shared this view. See, for example, "Statement by Foreign Minister Brandt to the Bundestag: Nonproliferation of Nuclear Weapons {Extracts}, February 1, 1967," in ibid.

46. See "Statement by Foreign Minister Brandt to the Bundestag on Proposed Nonproliferation Treaty, April 27, 1967," in *Documents on Disarmament, 1967,* 211–12.

47. Ibid.

48. See "Statement by the Nigerian Representative (Sule Kolo) to the Eighteen-Nation Disarmament Committee: Draft Nonproliferation Treaty [Extract], November 2, 1967," in U.S. Arms Control, *Documents on Disarmament, 1967,* 557–58.

49. See "Swiss Aide Memoire to the Co-Chairmen of the Eighteen-Nation Disarmament Committee: Draft Nonproliferation Treaty, November 17, 1967," in U.S. Arms Control, *Documents on Disarmament, 1967,* 573.

50. On that, this language meant that nonweapons nations might be compelled to withdraw if the weapons states did not live up to their pledge to disarm, see "Statement by the Swedish Representative (Myrdal) to the Eighteen-Nation Disarmament Committee: Nonproliferation of Nuclear Weapons, February 8, 1968"; "Statement by the Ethiopian Representative (Makonnen) to the First Committee of the General Assembly: Nonproliferation of Nuclear Weapons, May 6, 1968"; and "Statement by the Indian Representative (Husain) to the Eighteen-Nation Disarmament Committee: Nonproliferation of Nuclear Weapons, February 27, 1968," in U.S. Arms Control and Disarmament Agency, *Documents on Disarmament, 1968,* (Washington, D.C.: USGPO, 1969), 45, 116, 293–94.

51. See "Television Interview with Chancellor Kiesinger: Nonproliferation Negotiations [Extract], February 17, 1967"; and "Statement by Foreign Minister Brandt to the Bundestag on Proposed Nonproliferation Treaty, April 27, 1967," in U.S. Arms Control, *Documents on Disarmament, 1967,* 91, 215.

52. See "Statement by the Canadian Representative (Burns) to the Eighteen-Nation Disarmament Committee: Nonproliferation of Nuclear Weapons, August 3, 1967," in U.S. Arms Control, *Documents on Disarmament 1967,* 315.

53. "Statement by the British Representative (Hope) to the First Committee of the General Assembly, December 14, 1967," in U.S. Arms Control, *Documents on Disarmament, 1967,* 458.

54. See "Statement by the Indian Representative (Trivedi) to the Eighteen-Nation Disarmament Committee: Nonproliferation of Nuclear Weapons, September 28, 1967," in U.S. Arms Control, *Documents on Disarmament, 1967,* 432.

55. See, for example, Eldon V. C. Greenberg, *The NPT and Plutonium: Applica-*

tion of NPT Prohibitions to "Civilian" Nuclear Equipment, Technology and Materials Associated with Reprocessing and Plutonium Use (Washington, D.C.: Nuclear Control Institute, 1993), 18–19.

56. See "Statement by the Dutch Representative (Eschauzier) to the First Committee of the General Assembly: Nonproliferation of Nuclear Weapons {Extract}, May 6, 1968," in U.S. Arms Control, *Documents on Disarmament, 1968*, 295–96.

57. See "Statement by ACDA Director Foster to the First Committee of the General Assembly: Nonproliferation of Nuclear Weapons, November 9, 1966," in U.S. Arms Control, *Documents on Disarmament, 1968*, 721.

58. Department of State, Policy Planning Council, "After NPT, What?" May 28, 1968, NSF, Box 26, LBJL, as cited in Avner Cohen, *Israel and the Bomb* (New York: Columbia University Press, 1998).

59. See "Spanish Memorandum to the Co-Chairmen of the Eighteen-Nation Disarmament Committee, February 8, 1968," in U.S. Arms Control, *Documents on Disarmament, 1968*, 40; and "Mexican Working Paper Submitted to the Eighteen-Nation Disarmament Committee: Suggested Additions to Draft Nonproliferation Treaty, September 19, 1967," in *Documents on Disarmament, 1967*, 394–95.

60. For this interpretation, see Greenberg, *The NPT and Plutonium*, and Arthur Steiner, "Article IV and the 'Straightforward Bargain' " (PAN Paper 78–832–08), in Albert Wohlstetter et al., *Towards a New Consensus on Nuclear Technology*, vol. II (Supporting Papers, U.S. Arms Control and Disarmament Agency, ACDA Report No. PH-78–04–832–33).

61. See, for example, Richard K. Betts, *Nuclear Blackmail and Nuclear Balance* (Washington, D.C.: The Brookings Institution, 1987); Scott D. Sagan, *The Limits of Safety: Organizations, Accidents, and Nuclear Weapons* (Princeton, NJ: Princeton University Press, 1993); "More Will Be Worse," in Scott Sagan and Kenneth Waltz, *The Spread of Nuclear Weapons: A Debate* (New York: W. W. Norton, 1995), 47–91; and Bruce Blair, *Strategic Command and Control* (Washington, D.C.: The Brookings Institution, 1985), 83–240. Many of the problems highlighted in these works were first forecast in Albert Wohlstetter, "The Delicate Balance of Terror," *Foreign Affairs*, January 1959, 211–34.

62. See Albert Wohlstetter, "NATO and the N+1 Country," *Foreign Affairs* (April 1961): 355–87; Francois Heisbourg, "The Prospects for Nuclear Stability Between India and Pakistan," *Survival* (Winter 1998–99): 77–92; Neil Joeck, *Maintaining Nuclear Stability in South Asia*, Adelphi Paper 312 (Oxford: Oxford University Press for the IISS, 1997); and Clayton P. Bowen and Daniel Wovlven, "Command and Control Challenges in South Asia," *The Nonproliferation Review* (Spring–Summer 1999): 25–35.

63. For the last comprehensive economic forecast as to when such fuels might make economic sense, see, for example, Brian G. Chow and Kenneth A. Solomon, *Limiting the Spread of Weapon-Usable Fissile Materials* (Santa Monica, CA: The RAND Corporation, October 1993), 25–54.

64. See David Kay, "Detection and Denial: Iraq and Beyond," *The Washington Quarterly* 18, no. 1 (Winter 1995): 85–105.

65. See David Albright, *Separated Civil Plutonium Inventories: Current and Future Directions* (Washington, D.C.: Institute for Science and International Security, 2000); Chow and Solomon, *Limiting Fissile Materials*, xiv–xv; and Paul Leventhal,

"IAEA's Safeguards Shortcomings—A Critique" (Washington, D.C.: Nuclear Control Institute, September 12, 1994).

66. See Fritz W. Schmidt, "The Zangger Committee: Its History and Future Role," *The Nonproliferation Review* (Fall 1994), 38–44. For more detailed information on the history of the Zangger Committee, see the Federation of American Scientists website, www.fas.org/nuke/control/zangger/index.html.

67. For one of the earliest, most comprehensive critiques of the NPT and IAEA, which followed the Indian test explosion, see Albert Wohlstetter, et al., "The Military Potential of Civilian Nuclear Energy," *Minerva* (Autumn–Winter 1977): 387–538, which is an abridged version of a 1975 U.S. Arms Control and Disarmament Agency study that was subsequently published in full in 1979 by the University of Chicago Press as *Swords from Plowshares*.

5

Proliferation Technology Control Regimes

Shortly after India exploded its first nuclear device, the key nuclear supplier nations, led by the United States, met privately in London. The purpose of this November 1975 meeting was to see if the United States, the Soviet Union, Great Britain, France, Germany, Canada, and Japan could agree to restrain their exports of special nuclear materials, technology, and key equipment relating to plutonium reprocessing, uranium enrichment, and heavy water production. These goods, U.S. President Gerald Ford had publicly argued, ought not to be sold, especially to "regions of conflict and instability."[1] Other forms of safeguarded civilian nuclear technology, U.S. officials insisted, should only be sold to nations that—unlike India—had placed all of their nuclear activities under IAEA safeguards.

THE NUCLEAR SUPPLIERS GROUP

After two years of additional meetings, an agreement was struck and an organization, known as the Nuclear Suppliers Group (NSG) was created along with a set of nuclear export control rules known as "The Guidelines for Nuclear Transfers."[2] These guidelines were transmitted to the IAEA director general in January 1978. But it was understood from the start that the NSG went beyond what was called for either by the IAEA's statute or the NPT. France, a nonsignator of the NPT, was an NSG member. More important, the NSG's business, unlike that of the NPT or the IAEA, was secret and explicitly discriminatory: The group met privately on eight separate occasions through late 1977 and exchanged information about destinations that presented proliferation threats great enough to warrant barring them access to nuclear technology.

The organization worked when the supplier nations used it. Unfortunately, the opposite was also the case. The NSG clearly helped prevent French and Belgian sales of plutonium reprocessing technology and equipment to Pakistan and South Korea in the 1970s and of French enrichment equipment to Brazil in the early 1980s. It also gave the United States additional moral authority in blocking proposed French and British plutonium reprocessing assistance to Taiwan.[3] On the other hand, the NSG did little to block Swiss and German contracts made in the mid- and late 1970s to sell Brazil and Argentina plutonium reprocessing and enrichment technology, reactors, and heavy water plants. Nor was it effective in blocking French and Italian reactor and reprocessing sales during the same period to Iraq.[4]

After 1977, the full membership of the NSG stopped meeting. Embarrassing revelations about Saddam Hussein's nuclear weapons acquisition efforts, however, compelled it to meet again in March 1991. Hosted by the Dutch at the urging of the United States, this NSG gathering agreed to extend the organization's export guidelines to cover the type of nuclear-related dual-use items Saddam had used to build up his nuclear program prior to Desert Storm. The control list the NSG finally adopted was similar to that which the United States had long used to control its exports unilaterally. In 1992, the group also agreed not to make any significant new nuclear transfers to any nation unless the recipient agreed to place all of its nuclear activities facilities under IAEA safeguards.[5]

With these reforms, the NSG enjoyed a modest revival. Yet, beyond its performance in blocking sensitive nuclear exports, its most important contribution to nonproliferation has been that of a model for export control regimes in general. In fact, publication of the NSG's guidelines in 1978 was followed only a few years later by separate international negotiations to establish similar export control guidelines for missile and chemical and biological weapons-related technologies.

The prime objective for all these control efforts was to prevent the spread of strategic weapons to regions of instability. In this respect, their goal was similar to that which originally motivated negotiation of the NPT. Yet, the concern was not on how the further spread of strategic weapons capabilities might complicate UN disarmament negotiations, but rather on how such proliferation might put states in the world's war-prone regions on even more of a hair-trigger to pre-empt or destroy one another. Implicit to this focus was the cold-war worry—nearly realized in Korea, Vietnam, Suez, the Taiwan Straits, Lebanon, and Cuba—that major regional conflicts might draw either one or both of the superpowers in and produce a possible nuclear stand-off. Effective implementation of these control regimes, then, was aimed at reducing the prospect of such flash points.

The cold war also generated indirect political support for these control efforts. Although nonproliferation restraints were not designed to help fight the cold war, they served as a natural extension of longstanding multilateral East-West strategic technology export controls established decades before under an organization known as the Coordinating Committee, (CoCom). Like CoCom, which was targeted to retard the rate of military innovation among Warsaw Pact nations and China, these nonproliferation control regimes were intended to keep potential adversaries (including several Warsaw Pact client states—that is, Libya, Syria, Iran, Iraq, North Korea)—from fully developing their military potential. To the extent that the United States and its allies were already committed to the cold war and CoCom, then, they were naturally supportive of the various proliferation technology control regimes.[6]

In two key respects, however, these control efforts were much more informal than either CoCom or the NPT. Indeed, two of their defining features were the extent to which they consciously avoided binding unanimous decisions and the kind of universal membership characteristic of international treaty obligations. In fact, none of these efforts were treaties at all, but rather simultaneously announced national export control policies that were negotiated and agreed to by like-minded nations and subsequently adopted as national law among the member states. This informality was no accident. The creators of these regimes understood that it would be far more difficult to come up with an agreed list of destinations to which exports should be banned or controlled than there was under CoCom. They also understood that unlike CoCom's targeted Communist nations, the destinations of proliferation concern were likely to change. Finally, these regimes' loose construction made it easier to avoid the kinds of self-defeating trade-offs—the watering down of safeguards procedures and the offering of risky "peaceful" technology transfers, for example—that previously were required to secure final signatures to the NPT.

THE MISSILE TECHNOLOGY CONTROL REGIME AND THE AUSTRALIA GROUP

These informal, flexible features certainly were evident and openly discussed in negotiating the Missile Technology Control Regime (MTCR). This effort, officially launched in 1987, began with only like-minded, advanced, aerospace-supplying nations—the United States, the United Kingdom, France, Japan, Canada, and Italy—that had a common desire to restrict missile technology exports to "projects of concern."[7] Far from reflecting universal concerns about missile proliferation, though, the MTCR emerged directly from a re-evaluation of U.S. space technology transfer policies.

In fact, from the late 1950s on, the United States had actively shared rocket technology with nations, such as India and Brazil, under an Eisenhower-inspired initiative known as the Space for Peace Program. Under the National Aeronautics and Space Act of 1958, the United States urged the U.S. National Aeronautic and Space Administration (NASA) to share space technology internationally. At the end of the Ford administration, though, the U.S. Arms Control and Disarmament Agency (ACDA) began to re-evaluate the proliferation effects of this policy. This review continued under the Carter administration and resulted in an interagency study on missile proliferation, which opened up U.S. Department of Commerce files on past U.S. dual-use missile technology exports for analysis.[8]

From this study, two different missile nonproliferation policy options were proposed. The first was to offer missile technology assistance only to nations that agreed to limit their rocketry activities to peaceful purposes and to curtail their own exports of such technology. The second was to negotiate a multilateral missile technology control regime. The first recommendation was adopted late in the Carter administration and produced space cooperation talks with the Japanese and a bilateral space cooperation treaty, which was concluded with Tokyo in 1980. Similar talks were also begun with Brazil, which was working on a large rocket program of its own. Brazil wanted to buy U.S. solid-rocket fuel technology and filament winding equipment to make lightweight rocket casings. Brazilian officials refused, however, to drop their military rocket plans. In fact, the Vertical Launch System (VLS) program was tied to Brazil's ongoing nuclear weapons effort as a delivery system. This produced an impasse.

Conditioning further U.S. space assistance to India was no less frustrating. India was working on several large rocket programs that incorporated U.S. space technology and that were being run by the same scientific organizations responsible for India's unsafeguarded nuclear activities.[9] India, too, refused U.S. conditions on space cooperation. Its rocket program, however, was more ambitious. In 1980, it succeeded in launching a large space launch vehicle (the SLV-3). Shortly after this rocket's first test flight, American officials reversed course and began blocking specific, sensitive space technology exports to India.

These export denials, then, gave rise to the alternative policy option recommended in the original ACDA study—negotiating a multilateral missile technology export control agreement. Formally adopted by President Ronald Reagan in November 1982, this new policy required appealing to the world's key space technology supplier nations to deny nuclear-capable missiles and related technology to states lacking long-range missiles. The United States immediately began private negotiations to clarify what this common policy should be with the other G-7 nations (Canada, France, Germany, Italy, Japan, and the United Kingdom). These talks continued for nearly four years. By 1985, though, the United States and the G-7 had reached enough consensus on missile technology controls to adopt similar policies of export restraint. Finally on April 16, 1987, a common set of guidelines, known as the Missile Technology Control Regime (MTCR), was simultaneously announced publicly as national policy by all seven member states.

Like the NSG, which allowed a majority of nuclear transfers to be made to safeguarded nuclear programs, the MTCR explicitly permitted missile technology and hardware transfers so long as they were related to nonmilitary satellites, aircraft, and small, short-range tactical missiles (e.g., air defense missile and airplane launched air-to-air and air-to-ground missile systems). What the MTCR was geared to block were aerospace technology and hardware transfers that might contribute to the development of rockets or unmanned air vehicles capable of lifting a crude nuclear device strategic distances. After some discussion, the performance parameters of such "nuclear capable" missiles were pegged at systems that could lift a 500 kilogram payload (the weight of a crude, first-generation nuclear device) a minimum of 300 kilometers (i.e., the distance considered to be strategic in the Middle East and Korea, where nuclear-armed missiles might be bought, developed, or used).[10]

Again, fear of catalytic and accidental wars—the concern that originally prompted negotiation of the NPT—was back, this time with a regional focus. The worry was that the United States and its allies had little or no effective defenses against long-range missiles and that even missiles with limited ranges in regions such as the Middle East or Korea could dramatically increase instability and possibly spark a nuclear war. In keeping with this concern, MTCR guidelines were expanded in 1992 to "limit the risks of proliferation of weapons of mass destruction" (i.e., nuclear, chemical, and biological weapons). This was accomplished by discouraging the transfer of missile technology and hardware that MTCR member governments believed was intended for use in a missile designed to deliver chemical or biological warheads.[11]

This broadening of the MTCR reflected the enthusiasm most MTCR member states had already shown for controlling yet another strategic weapons concern—chemical and biological agents. The hardware and technology relating to these weapons were covered under a separate proliferation control effort named after its original national sponsor, the Australia Group (AG). Announced in June 1985, negotiations to create the AG began shortly after UN investigators substantiated Iraq's massive use of chemical weapons in its war against Iran. Initially, the AG included the top twenty Western biochemical-producing nations. Although it welcomed the eventual adoption of a chemical weapons convention, the AG also consciously avoided becoming a treaty obligation. Like the MTCR and the NSG, the AG met privately, exchanged intelligence about probable proliferators and export denials, and encouraged members to adhere to a set of export control guidelines over chemical weapons precursors, biological weapons-related organisms and toxins, and key production-related items.

SANCTIONS

By the late 1980s, the AG, NSG, and MTCR were all up and operating. What was missing, however, was any clear means for their enforcement. In the case of regime members who engaged in questionable export activities, the most these regimes called for were consultations. If one member considered exporting a controlled item to a given destination that another member had already denied, it was supposed to consult that member before proceeding to ensure that it did not undercut the denial. Whatever prospective exports member states chose not to talk about, though, frequently were shipped without mention. Nor were the strategic exports or imports of nonmembers something that these regimes could act on. These enforcement gaps were significant but they were tolerated until two nonproliferation scandals emerged: one following India's test explosion in 1974 and the other regarding Iraq's strategic arms build-up in the late 1980s.

After India's 1974 nuclear test, U.S. State Department officials claimed that no U.S.-approved nuclear assistance was used by India to make its explosive. Congress, though, was anxious to make clear its displeasure with this test and added a provision to the International Development Association Act in August 1974. It required U.S. officials to oppose international loans to "non-NPT states" that had developed nuclear explosives—that is, India. What made this legislation particularly timely were press reports that White House officials may have actually known that India was going to test more than two months before it did but chose to do nothing to block it.[12] Not surprisingly, executive branch officials resented the law and were only willing to do the bare minimum to implement it. Thus, on twenty-six separate occasions, U.S. State Department officials voted against proposed loans but chose to do nothing to sway other association members to do likewise.[13]

Congress was unhappy with this and soon had cause to act again. In response to congressional inquiries, Secretary of State Henry Kissinger in 1976 conceded that, contrary to earlier State Department statements, India had, in fact, used U.S.-approved heavy water exports to produce the plutonium it exploded in its first nuclear device. Worse yet, these U.S. exports were sent under safeguards that were so loose, India disputed it had violated any legal obligation in doing so.

To make sure this did not happen again and to slow Pakistan's nuclear efforts to catch up, Congress reacted to these revelations by passing a series of amendments to the U.S. Atomic Energy and Foreign Assistance acts. These amendments prohibited U.S. economic assistance, military aid or credits, arms exports, and military training to any nation that received or transferred nuclear reprocessing equipment or technology to any nonweapons state as defined by the NPT. In addition, they provided for a cut-off of such assistance to any nation that tested a nuclear device.[14] Nations that failed to place all of their nuclear activities and materials under IAEA safeguards or that had violated such safeguards were also targeted by Congress with a cut-off of Export-Import Bank loans and U.S.-controlled nuclear exports.[15] Although none of these nuclear sanctions would be triggered until the revival of India and Pakistan's nuclear weapons efforts in the 1990s, these amendments would effectively shape U.S. and allied nuclear cooperation, not only with India, but China and other non-NPT states, such as Argentina and Brazil.

The next wave of nonproliferation sanctions came nearly a decade later in the wake of Iraq's offensive use of chemicals against Iran and news that German defense contractors under the employ of the U.S. Defense Department were helping Argentina, Egypt, and Iraq develop an advanced ballistic missile known as the Condor II. This series of laws included the Missile Technology Control Act of 1990, the Chemical and Biological Weapons Control and Warfare Elimination Act of 1991, the Iran-Iraq Nonproliferation Act of 1992, and the Nuclear Proliferation Prevention Act of 1994.[16]

These bills put pressure on the executive branch to act against proliferators when there was credible evidence of bad behavior. They authorized the president to deprive any foreign entity or nation outside of the MTCR of U.S.-controlled munitions or dual-use commodities (items useful for both civilian and military purposes) if they supplied, received, or conspired to transfer controlled missile technology to nations not adhering to the MTCR. They also authorized sanctions against other nations' preparation for or initiation of chemical or biological weapons use, and against suppliers of advanced weaponry and related technology to Iran and Iraq. Finally, the Nuclear Proliferation Prevention Act of 1994 called for a series of sanctions including cutting off nuclear testing states' access to public and private U.S. financial institutions.[17]

Initially, the Bush administration resisted congressional adoption of these bills. The White House tried to deflect them by promulgating executive orders of its own. In addition, and shortly after the near export of an "uncontrolled" high-technology induction furnace to Iraq before

Desert Shield, the White House announced the Enhanced Proliferation Control Initiative (EPCI) and "catch all" controls. Under these regulations, even U.S. exports of unlisted items would require an export license (that the U.S. government could deny) if the exporter knew or was informed by the U.S. government that the export would help another nation develop a strategic weapon.[18]

Although substantial, these executive initiatives failed to deflect congressional demands for legislation. The reason why was the Gulf War and the White House's desire to justify it on the grounds of fighting proliferation. During most of the 1980s, the Reagan and Bush administrations and most Republicans and Democrats in Congress, in fact, favored Iraq over Iran and took a lax approach to restricting dual-use exports to Saddam Hussein. As became embarrassingly clear in House hearings held after the war, this resulted in the U.S. Commerce Department approving many dual-use items that went directly into Saddam's missile, chemical and nuclear programs.[19] When Saddam invaded Kuwait, though, the Bush administration deployed forces defensively in Saudi Arabia and urged the UN to impose trade sanctions, which seemed at odds with the administration's continued opposition to congressional nonproliferation sanctions.

Compounding this political awkwardness was the White House's decision in the late fall of 1990 to launch offensive military operations against Iraq. Sanctions now were deemed insufficient to persuade Saddam to leave Kuwait. Only offensive military action, Bush officials argued, could accomplish this. The problem was how to justify such action. By far the most publicly popular justification—and the one seized upon by the Bush administration—was that air and ground operations were the only way to destroy Saddam's strategic weapons projects. Once President George Bush committed the nation to wage ground operations against Saddam's strategic weapons programs, he reversed his opposition to Congress's proposed sanctions acts, and signed all of them into law.[20]

Backed with threat of these sanctions, the NSG, MTCR, and AG actually achieved a number of nonproliferation successes. As already noted, the NSG was instrumental in blocking sales and development of reprocessing plants in Taiwan, South Korea, and Pakistan. In addition, in the early 1990s, the United States persuaded South Korea, Taiwan, and South Africa to suspend their space launch vehicle programs; Argentina and Egypt to terminate their Condor II missile program; and Israel to end its missile exports to South Africa. In each of these cases, the U.S. diplomats depended heavily on the MTCR and the threat of sanctions.

REGIME EXPANSION AND DECONTROLS

By the early 1990s, America's reliance on export controls and sanctions to promote nonproliferation reached its apex. The key reason why was the collapse of the Soviet Union. Without the cold war and the prospect of a global conflict, public support for continuing these restraints began to wane. Initially, the war against Saddam Hussein and the impetus it gave to expand existing strategic controls and sanctions, obscured this point. Besides Iraq, most American officials thought it was clear who the key trouble states were—Iran, North Korea, Syria, and Libya. Yet, without the cold war, America's allies were no longer so opposed to doing business with these nations. Ignoring this point, the United States tried to get its allies to back strengthening controls and sanctions. In the long run, this effort proved to be disappointing.

The first indication that it would be difficult to fortify existing controls came with U.S. efforts to expand membership in the MTCR, AG, and NSG. After a spat of embarrassing press reports detailing how the West assisted Saddam Hussein's strategic weapons programs, the United States and its allies were understandably anxious to prevent the reoccurrence of such aid.[21] There was little interest, though, in making the existing control regimes more discriminatory or punitive. Instead, U.S. officials chose to enlarge them by making AG, MTCR, and NSG membership as universal as possible. Yet, most like-minded nations—for example, NATO and European Union members—already were members of these control efforts. The only significant membership prospects left, then, were former Warsaw Pact nations and known proliferators.

This complicated matters. To get large nations such as Russia, China, and Brazil to stop proliferating, the United States and its allies felt they had to give them incentives. In specific, the United States and its allies offered these nations freer access to controlled strategic technology and reduced exposure to U.S. sanctions if they would promise to end their proliferating ways.

This campaign to expand the regimes was popular. The European Union, in fact, was already loosening its trade controls and trying to increase investment in Russia and Eastern Europe. As such, relaxing regime membership standards to permit these nations to join was welcome. Moreover, with the economic recession in the United States, anything that promised increased exports and employment enjoyed public support. Indeed, the streamlining of export controls and the substitution of unnecessary controls with generalized (preapproved) export licensing procedures were all measures that industry now demanded and that the United States and other key democracies endorsed.[22] Finally, with the end of the cold war, both U.S. businessmen and diplomats—

anxious to engage Russia and China—were beginning to chafe under the constraints of nonproliferation export control sanctions laws that Congress had just passed.

At the time the United States and its allies were expanding the membership of the AG, MTCR, and NSG, then, they were just as aggressive in decontrolling their high-technology exports and doing so frequently in the name of nonproliferation. Late in 1992, for example, the State Department decided to allow U.S. exporters to ship chemical precursors to AG members without having to secure a U.S. export license. The idea here was not just to reduce licensing requirements on U.S. exports, but to reward AG members for their willingness to adhere to international nonproliferation norms. This decision was also informed by the judgment that export controls over chemicals were unlikely ever to be all that effective and were becoming less so as more nations mastered the techniques of producing their own precursor chemicals.

About the same time as these actions were taken, the Bush administration also decided to allow U.S. satellites to be launched from Russian rockets and to waive restrictions on similar launchings out of China. Although private demand for additional commercial satellite launch capacity was a key factor behind granting these waivers, getting Russia and China to pledge adherence to the MTCR guidelines was also presented as a stated objective. In addition, the Bush administration adjusted upward the levels at which exports of personal and advanced computers would be controlled to keep these controls relevant.[23]

Finally, and perhaps most important, the Bush administration made it clear that CoCom controls against Russia, Eastern Europe, and China would soon become a thing of the past. In fact, shortly after the fall of the Soviet Union, CoCom members agreed to reduce the number of items the organization would control. This decision was followed by additional efforts to streamline CoCom's control lists and an announcement in November 1992 (made at America's urging), that the organization would give way to a new body, the CoCom Cooperation Forum, which would include the former Warsaw Pact nations as members. The idea here was to try to convert CoCom from an East-West control organization into a nonproliferation control regime while increasing the former Eastern bloc's access to Western high technology.[24]

These Bush initiatives were modest but nonetheless set the tone for what was to follow: the total elimination of CoCom in 1994; the transformation of the NSG, AG, and MTCR from like-minded discriminatory organizations to norm-based efforts that increased members' access to technology; the aggressive decontrol of national export controls; and a decline in support for unilateral proliferation sanctions.

President Bush, of course, lost his bid for re-election in 1992 before these decontrol results were realized. President Bill Clinton, however, more than picked up from where the Bush administration left off. Clinton's presidential campaign had favored efforts to boost U.S. exports. But it also was committed to promoting nonproliferation. The question was how to do both. The answer, outlined in campaign policy papers published just prior to Clinton's election, was to coordinate the decontrol of exports with increased nonproliferation diplomacy. Relaxing formal export licensing requirements, it was argued, should be balanced by making such trade more transparent and by fostering international nonproliferation norms to prevent this technology from being used for military purposes.[25]

How was this to be done? First, the nuclear powers had to demonstrate their willingness to de-emphasize their reliance on weapons of mass destruction. This required that they further reduce their own arsenals, end nuclear testing, complete a convention controlling chemical weapons-related activities, and strengthen international restraints over biological weapons agents. Second, instead of denying nations access to sensitive technology (particularly dual-use items and know-how), greater attention would be paid to controlling nations' intentions to misapply it. All of these proposed efforts were to reflect a change from America's cold war strategies of containment and rivalry with the Warsaw Pact to cooperative security with all strategic weapons states.[26]

INTEGRATING RUSSIA INTO A NEW MTCR

These ideas were attractive. In practice, though, they were difficult to achieve. This became clear almost immediately with Russia and China and U.S. efforts to get them to end their proliferation activities. The first step taken toward this end was President Clinton's announcement of a new U.S. missile nonproliferation policy (Presidential Review Directive 8) at the UN General Assembly on September 27, 1993.[27] Under this new policy, instead of opposing the export of space launch vehicles (SLVs) or SLV-related exports (technology that was interchangeable with intercontinental ballistic missile technology) the United States would now consider such exports to MTCR members. More importantly, the United States would approve such exports for nations with the very best nonproliferation credentials as a way to induce more countries to sign on to the MTCR and other nonproliferation understandings. As such, the prime objective of U.S. missile nonproliferation policy now was to secure nations' pledges to "abandon *offensive* ballistic missile programs." Opposing the spread of missile capabilities *per se*—the Bush and Reagan policy—in short, was *passé*. Controlling for intentions was key.[28]

Initially, the only matters affected by this announcement were a series of U.S. export licenses covering the release of U.S. SLV hardware to Australia, Spain, and Italy, all of whom were MTCR members. Previously, the Bush administration only approved technical discussions about these possible transfers. Nothing more was permitted because the U.S. Defense Department feared that actually approving these exports would lead to the United States having to do the same with all MTCR members including Argentina, which the United States had just persuaded to abandon its large rocket program. Congress shared these reservations and formally objected to Clinton's nonproliferation policy announcement in a joint congressional resolution passed late in 1993.[29]

So matters stood until the issue of Russian and Brazilian membership in the MTCR was raised sixteen months later in 1995. Russia had a poor record of adhering to MTCR guidelines. In fact, a Russian export firm, Glavkosmos, had been sanctioned under U.S. law under the Bush administration in 1992 for having exported critical missile items and production technology to India. Even after Clinton administration officials terminated these sanctions in 1993, they blocked Russia's admission into the MTCR pending Russian confession to twelve other MTCR guidelines violations that the U.S. intelligence agencies knew about.

One of these missile transgressions was Russia's shipment of rocket casing technology to Brazil's SLV project. Since the late 1980s, the United States had identified this Brazilian program as a missile proliferation project of concern and had curtailed U.S. and other MTCR nations' missile technology exports to it for fear that they might get re-exported to Libya, Iran, or Iraq.[30] The European Union (EU), however, wanted to increase its high technology commerce with Moscow. In March 1994, the EU worked with the United States to dissolve CoCom and to negotiate a successor organization, formally known as the Wassenaar Arrangement on Export Controls for Conventional Arms and Dual-Use Goods and Technologies. Although broad in scope, this organization, announced in December 1995 with Russia as a member, became hardly more than a forum to exchange information on exports already shipped. There was no agreed list of proscribed destinations, no CoCom-like mechanism to preview or veto other members' exports, and no proscription against undercutting other members' specific export denials. It was successful, however, in helping to remove political objections to granting Russia freer access to advanced Western technology.[31]

There was, however, one problem. Most aerospace exports were not covered by the Wassenaar Arrangement. As a result, Russia and the EU placed considerable pressure on the United States also to agree to admit Russia into the MTCR. This, the United States in principle agreed to do late in 1994. A key condition for Russia's admission, though, was for Russia to admit that it had engaged in several missile proliferation activities (referred to as the Dirty Dozen). Russia was finally admitted after the Clinton administration took two actions in June and July 1995. First, the White House waived sanctions that U.S. law had required against

Russia for its illicit missile technology sales to Brazil. Second, the U.S. backed Russian MTCR membership after State Department officials shared intelligence with the Russian Foreign Ministry concerning the twelve known MTCR transgressions.

In bringing Russia into the MTCR, the Clinton administration also proposed to bring in Brazil. Clinton's proposal immediately raised congressional objections that Russia would then be legally free to sell Brazil the very rocket technology that the MTCR was designed to help block and that even U.S. missile technology might end up there.[32] The EU, after all, was transferring MTCR technology license-free within its membership, and the Clinton administration had already set the precedent by making such transfers license-free to MTCR members it trusted. Also, under U.S. missile technology sanctions law, MTCR nations could not be sanctioned for transferring missile technology to other MTCR members.[33]

Beyond this, Congress was upset with Brazil's admission to the MTCR because of the policy precedent it would set concerning U.S. SLV exports. Prior to the Clinton administration, it had been U.S. and MTCR policy not to admit any nation trying to develop large missiles. To become an MTCR member, such nations first had to abandon such projects (as in the case of Argentina and South Africa, both of which had to terminate their large rocket programs before being backed for MTCR membership). President Clinton's willingness to support Brazil's membership as soon as it passed missile export control legislation without terminating its large rocket program, though, made it clear that this policy was being renounced.

Indeed, as the administration's critics saw it, the president's decision to let Brazil join the MTCR undermined the MTCR's discriminatory character and made it more like the concessionary, universalistic nonproliferation regimes (e.g., the NPT) that it was originally designed to avoid. It clearly shifted the regime's emphasis away from blocking the spread of technical capabilities back toward the NPT-like task of offering access to sensitive technology in exchange for pledges of nonproliferation intent.[34]

TRYING TO GET RUSSIA TO COOPERATE

Again, this reversion to an NPT formula was defended by U.S. officials as being necessary to bolster international sentiment against proliferation. Clearly, it was becoming increasingly difficult to deny nations access to dual-use technology useful for making weapons capable of mass destruction as more suppliers came online. Critics, however, voiced concern. Wouldn't including both proliferation suppliers and consumers into organizations that had relatively free trade in sensitive technology simply turn existing proliferation technology denial regimes into proliferation breeding grounds? Wouldn't making such proliferators members in good standing render any effective sanctioning of proliferation violations nearly impossible?[35]

In time, these fears were realized, particularly with Russia. The White House, in fact, was eager to showcase Russia as a test bed for cooperative security—a new approach that contrasted with the cold war containment policies of armed rivalry, trade controls, and distrust. As an incentive to promote better Russian nonproliferation behavior, U.S. officials not only avoided sanctioning Russian proliferation activities, but rewarded Moscow for nonproliferation pledges that Moscow subsequently broke.

This unhealthy pattern began with U.S.-Russian missile nonproliferation negotiations in 1993 over Russia's continued missile assistance to India. As already noted, the Bush administration had sanctioned Glavkosmos, a Russian missile export firm. Glavkosmos had contracted with the Indian Scientific Research Organization (ISRO) to sell India several cryogenic upper stages along with the production technology necessary to produce them. Under the MTCR, the transfer of missile production technology (hardware or know-how) is strictly forbidden. More important, the Russian upper stage technology could be used to help India extend the range of its rockets to reach Beijing and to improve the accuracy of its missiles.[36]

Initially, the Russians refused to terminate the deal. To get Moscow to change its mind, U.S. officials offered to expand the number of U.S.-made satellite launches Russia could bid on and to fund Russia's participation in U.S. space cooperative projects if Moscow would relent. In July 1993, it did: President Boris Yeltsin promised President Clinton to reconfigure Russia's contract with ISRO by November 1, 1993, so it would exclude any transfers of production technology.

The problem was getting the Russians to fully implement this understanding. Between July and October, ISRO personnel were at the Russian rocket manufacturing plants that made the cryogenic stages. Indian officials claimed that Russia transferred more than "4/5ths" of the sanctioned production technology. Then, India's minister of state in the Department of Atomic Energy and Space confirmed the worst. Contrary to the Russians' pledge not to transfer technical manuals that would permit India to produce its own cryogenic rocket engines, Russia had sent ISRO in September 1993 all the "drawings of the engine" ISRO needed to produce the engines within a few years.[37]

All of these missile technology transfers clearly violated the MTCR and the spirit of the Yeltsin-Clinton agreement (which had been finalized in September 1993) but they were forgiven on the legal grounds that the United States had allowed Russia until November 1, 1993, to reconfigure its contract with ISRO. Yet, evidence soon emerged that the Russians continued to transfer missile production technology to ISRO well after this date. In specific, the U.S. House Science Committee discovered that one of Russia's leading space launch firms, Salyut/Khrunichev, was still training ISRO personnel about the details of rocket launch integration as late as June 1994. In a private September 1994 meeting, the committee's chairman brought this information to the attention of Vice President Al Gore, who chaired a series of meetings on nonproliferation and space policy issues with his Russian counterpart, Prime Minister Victor Chernomyrdin.[38]

Instead of sanctioning Moscow as authorized by U.S. law, the White House decided to proceed with its program of positive incentives. This included at least $400 million (what the Russians said terminating the ISRO contract cost them) to the Russian Space Agency (RSA) for joint work on the International Space Station and Russia's space laboratory Mir. It also included approval of over $500 million dollars worth of Russian launchings of U.S.-made satellites, and membership in the MTCR. In addition, in the nuclear field, the United States began spending hundreds of millions of dollars to help Russia convert its strategic weapons complexes to peaceful purposes. The hope was that by paying Russia to demilitarize and to curb its proliferation activities, the United States could directly reduce the strategic weapons threats Moscow posed.

In the context of the administration's cooperative security effort, nonproliferation experts celebrated the Gore-Chernomyrdin agreement as a significant nonproliferation success.[39] And for a while, Russia's continued proliferation activities seemed tolerable. When Russia officially transferred Scud missiles to the new nation of Armenia in violation of the MTCR, White House officials were quick to note that the missiles had actually been deployed in Armenia before the Soviet Union's collapse.[40] Later, when news broke of Russian missile guidance sets being shipped to Iraq in 1995, U.S. State Department officials investigated the transfers, failed to establish a direct link to the Russian government, and judged them to be an aberration.[41] Far more disturbing was Russia's announcement of nuclear cooperation with Iran. But after appealing to Moscow and banning U.S. oil investments in Iran and Iranian imports to the United States, Russia was persuaded to drop the most objectionable aspects of its nuclear dealings with Tehran—a gas centrifuge uranium enrichment plant and a heavy-water reactor optimized for plutonium production. Continued Russian nuclear and missile technology transfers to China, of course, were still a problem, but China already was a weapons state and, in any case, had been buying Russian strategic technology for some time.[42] However tenuous cooperative security with Russia seemed, its proponents, then, were insistent that it was still working.[43]

Early in 1997, however, revelations concerning Russian assistance to Iran's missile programs all but demolished such optimism. U.S. intelligence officials knew that Russia had helped Iran on a single-stage rocket of North Korean design known as the Shahab-3. What they did not know was that Russia had become the prime contractor for developing a new, multi-stage 2,000 kilometer-range system for Iran known as the Shahab-4. The Israelis, who had detailed information on this program (which included the transfer of technicians, wind tunnels, missile test stands, guidance systems, and Russian SS-4 strategic rocket stages), made sure they found out. Just days before Russian Prime Minister Victor Chernomyrdin and Vice President Gore were to hold their next space nonproliferation summit, Israel sent General Amos Gilad, director of research for Israeli military intelligence, to Washington. Gilad briefed the U.S. Central Intelligence Agency, key congressional staff on Russia's missile assistance to Iran, and—after first leaking this information to the press—Vice President Gore.[44]

These disclosures put supporters of cooperative security with Russia on the defensive. President Clinton responded by appointing a special envoy, former Ambassador Frank Wisner, to try to convince Yuri Koptev, head of the Russian Space Agency (RSA), to stem Russia's missile assistance to Iran. But after an intensive year of talks, Wisner made little progress. Then came a public insult: The Russian press revealed that the RSA was playing a key role in coordinating the recruitment and travel of Russian missile engineers to Tehran.[45] Congress, already poised to sanction Moscow, easily passed such legislation June 9, 1998. The president, however, was still anxious to work to promote nonproliferation cooperation with the Russians. On June 23 he vetoed the legislation and instead imposed limited sanctions three weeks later against those entities that the Russian government agreed were involved.[46]

Although politically adroit in the short run (Congress decided against trying to override the veto), the president's sanctions actions, unfortunately, had no effect on continued U.S.-Russian space cooperation and commerce and did little to slow continued Russian missile assistance to Iran. In fact, none of the Russian aerospace entities the White House had targeted conducted any business with U.S. firms. On the other hand, the RSA, which by 1999 had taken in well over a billion dollars of NASA's budget to work on the space station, was conspicuously missing from the president's sanctions list.

This was unacceptable to Congress. Instead of calling for mandatory sanctions, it decided instead to secure a much more modest goal—suspending U.S. payments to the most important known Russian missile proliferator to Iran, the RSA, until the president could certify that it had stopped proliferating.[47] This more moderate approach, which merely suspended direct U.S. subsidies to specific proliferators rather than punishing them or related parties, was hailed by all sides as a model for future nonproliferation legislation. It passed unanimously in the House and Senate and, after initially fighting it, President Clinton signed it into law claiming that it reflected his opposition to traditional mandatory sanctions.[48]

CHINA AND FURTHER DECONTROLS

Given these results, Congress's fears in 1995 that bringing Russia into the MTCR would make it nearly impossible to sanction it for its proliferating behavior seemed justified. Also as Congress had feared, other nations, including Ukraine and South Korea refused to join the MTCR unless they were brought in with the privileges the United States had afforded Russia or Brazil—that is, freedom to make either long-range missiles or SLVs of their own.

This only made Congress more anxious to keep the executive branch from bringing China, one of the world's other great proliferators, into the MTCR. The White House, however, was committed to bringing China into as many nonproliferation regimes as it could. Indeed, the State Department went out of its way to secure pledges of better nonproliferation behavior from Beijing while engaging China with trade in sensitive high technology commodities (including U.S. chemical production equipment, satellite integration information, and nuclear-related technology and equipment). The idea here was to show trust and to demonstrate to China that good nonproliferation behavior produced commercial dividends.[49]

By its second term, the Clinton administration claimed that its approach was succeeding. China, it noted, had ratified or signed the Nuclear Nonproliferation Treaty, the Chemical Weapons Convention, and the Comprehensive Test Ban and was adhering to the MTCR guidelines. However, the price for such progress was an embarrassing level of strategic commerce with some of China's worst proliferating entities. Thus, the White House approved over $21 million in U.S. government guaranteed exports of controlled chemical production equipment to the Nanjing Chemical Industrial Group before the president finally sanctioned the firm in 1996 for violating the Chemical Weapons Convention. Similarly, from 1994 through 1997, U.S. officials approved over a billion dollars in guaranteed U.S. government loans to U.S. firms exporting nuclear-related goods and services to Chinese entities (e.g., Chinese National Nuclear Corporation) known to be assisting Iranian and Pakistani nuclear weapons efforts.[50] As for the Comprehensive Test Ban, China signed this in 1996 but only after it had gained increased access to U.S. nuclear research facilities and much more advanced U.S. computers. The year it signed, China conducted a series of nuclear tests. These were of advanced warheads whose designs U.S. officials feared were stolen from U.S. nuclear weapons laboratories. Finally, from 1989 through 1998, the

United States continued to transfer U.S.-made satellites to China's Great Wall Industries despite warnings that this might enhance China's missile capabilities and assist a key Chinese missile proliferator. Indeed, among this trade's benefactors (worth nearly a billion dollars in hard currency) were the very firms that had been helping Pakistani, North Korean, and Iranian missile programs and that were working to improve China's strategic missile force.[51]

None of this did much to endear Congress to the administration's approach. In 1998, almost everything seemed to go wrong. Iran tested the Shahab-3 missile with Russian, Chinese, and North Korean assistance. India tested nuclear weapons and long-range rockets with Russian help. Pakistan replied with nuclear tests of its own and deployed rockets developed with Chinese and North Korean help. North Korea was suspected of having violated its NPT pledge and its 1994 agreement with the United States not to develop nuclear weapons and, then in August, it fired a three-stage intercontinental-range-capable rocket over Japan.

India and Pakistan's nuclear tests in 1998 immediately triggered automatic U.S. economic sanctions. But by year's end, both the White House and Congress had all but vitiated the most substantive restrictions on U.S. technology exports to India and on Indian financial transactions in the U.S.[52] In addition, two major congressional investigations, one a congressionally mandated review of the ballistic missile threat chaired by former Secretary of Defense Donald Rumsfeld and another congressional investigation of Chinese theft of U.S. missile and nuclear weapons information only further hardened congressional opinion against the efficacy of traditional nonproliferation export controls and sanctions.[53]

Trade sanctions, it was argued, generally did not work and hurt U.S. exporters more than the proliferators they were directed against. It might make sense to continue to control U.S. exports for the limited purpose of upholding America's nonproliferation moral standing. Certainly, U.S. exports and aid should not be used to subsidize known proliferators. But beyond this, there was a limit to how much such controls could accomplish: At the height of the cold war, the U.S. government carefully reviewed over 100,000 dual-use exports; by 1999 that number had declined to less than 9,000.

Moreover, with the cold war over, continued trade vigilance was unlikely. Indeed, besides belated efforts to monitor satellite exports to China and foreign visitors at U.S. national weapons laboratories, congressional critics of the administration's loose technology controls were largely at a loss as to what to recommend. Not surprisingly, none of the additional decontrols the White House announced in 1999 over satellite imagery, encryption, and advanced computer exports were effectively opposed.

There was some interest on Capitol Hill and elsewhere in developing new sanctions against proliferation.[54] Yet, the bulk of administration critics increasingly turned their attention to deploying missile defenses and to the general task of deterring and defending against strategic weapons proliferation that had already occurred or was deemed inevitable in North Africa, the Middle East, Southwest Asia, and the Far East. In this regard, their views were hardly different from those voiced by senior defense officials at the start of the Clinton administration. Their conclusion after reviewing the proliferation scene was much the same: Ultimately, the best the United States could do against the spread of strategic weapons was to try to counter it militarily.

NOTES

1. Support of the Nuclear Suppliers Group, in fact, was part of a larger U.S. nuclear nonproliferation initiative launched by President Ford after the Indian test explosion to oppose the commercialization of plutonium reprocessing in the United States and other nations and to restrict the use of nuclear weapons-usable fuels in general. This policy was publicly announced nearly a year later. See Gerald Ford, "Statement on Nuclear Policy," October 28, 1976, reprinted in U.S. Congress, Congressional Research Service, *Nuclear Proliferation Factbook* (Washington, D.C.: USGPO, 1995), 48–62.

2. The Nuclear Suppliers Group is also referred to as the London Suppliers Group, after the location of its meetings.

3. On these points, see Leonard Spector, *Nuclear Proliferation Today* (New York: Vintage Books, 1984), 78–83, 262–63, 341–43, 447–51.

4. See Ibid., 166–73, 209–211, 239–44.

5. See a monograph by Roland Timerbaev, "A Major Milestone in Controlling Nuclear Exports" (Monterey, CA: Center for Russian and Eurasian Studies, Monterey Institute of International Studies, 1992); Tariq Rauf, Mary Beth Nikitin, and Jenni Rissanen, *Inventory of International Nonproliferation Organizations and Regimes* (Monterey, CA: Center for Nonproliferation Studies, August 2000), 31–37; and Richard T. Cupitt, *Reluctant Champions: U.S. Presidential Policy and Strategic Export Controls* (New York: Routledge Press, 2000), 150–51.

6. For a concise history of CoCom and its relations to U.S. and multilateral proliferation technology controls, see U.S. Congress, House, Select Committee on U.S. National Security and Military/Commercial Concerns with the Peoples Republic of China, *U.S. National Security and Military/Commercial Concerns with the Peoples Republic of China*, vol. III (Washington, D.C.: USGPO, May 1999), 6–19.

7. For a comprehensive history of the MTCR written by one of its key negotiators, see Richard H. Speier, "The Missile Technology Control Regime: Case Study of a Multilateral Negotiation," a paper submitted to the United States Institute of Peace under grant # SG-31-95, November 1995. (Available upon request from USIP)

8. See Maurice Eisenstein, "Third World Missiles and Nuclear Proliferation," *The Washington Quarterly* (Summer 1982), 112–15. Mr. Eisenstein was in charge of the ACDA study during the Carter years.

9. See Gary Milhollin, "India's Missiles—With a Little Help from Our Friends," *Bulletin of the Atomic Scientists* (May 1989); 31–36.

10. See note 7; White House, "Missile Technology Control Regime: Fact Sheet to Accompany Public Announcement," The White House, Office of the Press Secretary, Santa Barbara, California, April 16, 1987; and Richard H. Speier, "The Missile Technology Control Regime," in *Chemical Weapons and Missile Proliferation*, edited by Trevor Findlay (Boulder, CO: Lynne Rienner Publishers, 1991), 115–21.

11. For revision and narrative descriptions, see U.S. Department of State, "Department of State Daily Press Briefing, January 7, 1993"; and K. Scott McMahon and Dennis M. Gormley, "Controlling the Spread of Land-Attack Cruise Missiles," in *Fighting Proliferation: New Concerns for the 1990s*, edited by Henry Sokolski (Maxwell Air Force Base, AL: Air University Press, 1996), 148–50.

12. Thomas O'Toole, "Earlier Try of Indian Bomb Told," *The Washington Post*, July 13, 1974, A3.

13. See Spector, *Nuclear Proliferation Today*, 36–37.

14. See The International Security Assistance Act of 1977, Section 12 (Public Law 95–92; 91 Stat. 620); The International Security Assistance Act of 1978, Section 10(b)(4) (Public Law 95–384; 92 Stat. 735); The International Security Assistance Act of 1981, Section 735 (Public Law 97–113; 95 Stat. 1561); and The International Security and Development Cooperation Act of 1981, section 737(c) (Public Law 97–113; 95 Stat. 1562), all of which are reprinted in U.S. Congress, Congressional Research Service, *Nuclear Proliferation Fact Book*, 280–81.

15. See Amendment to the Export-Import Bank Act of 1945, Section 2(b)(1)(A) (Public Law 95–143; 91 Stat. 1210) passed October 26, 1977, and Nuclear Non-Proliferation Act of 1978 (Public Law 95–242; 92 Stat. 120) reprinted in *Nuclear Proliferation Fact Book*, 296 ff.

16. For a review of this wave of U.S. nonproliferation legislation, see Zachary Davis et al., *Proliferation Control Regimes: Background and Status* (Washington, D.C.: U.S. Congressional Research Service, 1995).

17. See Control of Missiles and Missile Equipment or Technology, Sec. 1703 of the National Defense Authorization Act for Fiscal Year 1991 (Public Law 101–510; 104 Stat. 1745), 22 U.S.C. 2797; the Chemical and Biological Weapons Control and Warfare Elimination Act of 1991, Title II of Public Law-182–182 (H.R. 1724), 105 Stat. 1222, approved December 4, 1992, 22 U.S.C. 5601; the Iran-Iraq Arms Nonproliferation Act of 1992, Title XVI, Public Law 102–484, 50 U.S.C. 1701 note; and the Nuclear Proliferation Prevention Act of 1994, Title VIII of the Foreign Relations Authorization Act, Fiscal Years 1994 and 1995, Public Law 103–236.

18. See Cupitt, *Reluctant Champions*, 141–42.

19. See U.S. Congress, House, Committee on Foreign Affairs, *United States Exports of Sensitive Technology to Iraq, Hearings before the Subcommittee on International Economic Policy and Trade*, 102nd Cong., 1st sess., April 8 and May 22, 1991; and U.S. Congress, House, The Committee on Urban Affairs, Banking, and Finance, *H.R. 4803, the Non-Proliferation of Weapons of Mass Destruction and Regulatory Improvement Act of 1992, Hearings on H.R. 4803*, 102nd Cong., 2nd sess., May 8, 1992.

20. For an excellent account of the relation between the war against Iraq and passage of these acts, see Cupitt, *Reluctant Champions*, 118–57.

21. Congress also was most emphatic that membership and adherence to ex-

isting control regimes needed to be expanded. See, for example, U.S. Congress, House, Committee on Government Operations, *Strengthening the Export Licensing System*, H. Rept. 102–137, 102nd Cong., 1st sess., July 2, 1991.

22. See, for example, The National Association of Manufacturers, *Export Control Reform: A Key to U.S. Export Success: Policy Recommendations* (Washington, D.C.: National Association of Manufacturers, June 1993), and Panel on the Future Design and Implementation of U.S. National Security Export Controls, *Finding Common Ground: U.S. Export Controls in a Changed Global Environment* (Washington, D.C.: National Academy Press, 1991).

23. See the concise history of these decontrols detailed in U.S. Congress, House, *Concerns with the People's Republic of China*, Vol. III, 55–60, 64–65.

24. See note 6 and Cupitt, *Reluctant Champions*, 154–55.

25. See Ashton B. Carter, William J. Perry, and John D. Steinbruner, *A New Concept of Cooperative Security* (Washington, D.C.: The Brookings Institution, 1992), 33–41. Also see Ad Hoc Working Group on Non-Proliferation and Arms Control, *Non-Proliferation and Arms Control: Issues and Options for the Clinton Administration* (Washington, D.C.: Ad Hoc Working Group on Non-Proliferation and Arms Control, January 1993); and Cupitt, *Reluctant Champions*, 160.

26. Ibid.

27. See White House, "President's Nonproliferation and Export Control Policy: Fact Sheet," September 27, 1993.

28. See John J. Fialka, "Nonproliferation Efforts Face Obstacles from North Korea, China, Capitol Hill," *The Wall Street Journal*, August 16, 1993, A-10; Douglas Frantz, "U.S. May Ease Export of Rocket Technology," *The Los Angeles Times*, August 10, 1993, 1; and Ben Iannotta, "Administration to Relax Rocket Export Rules," *Space News*, August 16–22, 1993, 1.

29. See U.S. Congress, *The Congressional Record*, August 6, 1993, pp. S 10935–36.

30. See U.S. Congress, House, Committee on Government Operations, *Strengthening the Export Licensing*, 27–29.

31. See Cupitt, *Reluctant Champions*, 174; Rauf, et al., *Inventory*, 28–30; and U.S. Congress, House, *Military Commercial Concerns with the People's Republic of China*, Vol. III., 14–17.

32. See, for example, U.S. Congress, *The Congressional Record*, August 1, 1995, pp. H8158–59; U.S. Congress, Senate, *The National Defense Authorization Act of FY 1996*, Section 1052, National Security Implications of United States Export Control Policy; and Jeffrey Smith, "U.S. Waives Objection to Russian Missile Technology Sale to Brazil," *The Washington Post*, June 8, 1995, A23.

33. Or, indeed, any nation. Under the law, if an MTCR member has no knowledge of an illicit export, it can plead ignorance as a defense (as Russia successfully did, for example, early in 1996 in response to revelations that Russian gyroscopes had found their way to Jordan on their way to Iraq). Moreover, even if an MTCR nation knowingly exports missile technology to another country, U.S. law exempts it from sanctions so long as it can claim that it believed the export to be compliant with MTCR guidelines.

34. A high-level Clinton official privately noted that with the Australia Group (AG) even modest efforts to increase adherence could backfire. As part of the AG's effort to expand its influence, the group began briefing nonmembers in

1993 on how to adhere to AG controls. Chinese officials were briefed on what the threshold amounts of various precursors were to specific trouble destinations that would concern the AG and the United States. Well after these briefings, China continued to sell precursor chemicals to dubious end users but now, this U.S. official noted, in amounts (per shipment) just below AG thresholds. In addition, if China became an AG member, this official noted that it could import precursor chemicals from AG members license-free, thus making the subsequent reshipment of these precursors through third party cut-outs extremely difficult to track.

35. On this point see Richard Speier, "An NPT for Missiles?" in *Fighting Proliferation: New Concerns for the 1990s*, edited by Henry Sokolski (Maxwell Air Force Base, AL: Air University Press, 1996), 57–74; and Henry Sokolski, "Curbing Proliferation's Legitimization," *Nonproliferation Review*, (Winter 1995); 1–4.

36. See U.S. Department of State, Office of the Assistant Secretary of State for Public Affairs, Margaret Tutwiller, "Russian Sale of Rocket Engine to India," May 11, 1992, and note 23 above.

37. See Vivek Raghuvanshi, "Russia, India Discuss Cryogenic Contract," *Space News*, November 15–28, 1993; John Wallach, "Clinton-Yeltsin Pledges Unlock Missile Dispute," *Hearst Publications*, July 26–August 6, 1993; and Reuters News Service, "Russia Not to Give Rocket Technology, India Says," July 25, 1994.

38. See Henry Sokolski, "Space Technology Transfers and Missile Proliferation," in *Report of the Commission to Assess the Ballistic Missile Threat to the United States*, July 15, 1998, Pursuant to Public Law 201, 104th Congress, Appendix III, Unclassified Working Papers, 303–15.

39. See, for example, Alexander A. Pikayev, Leonard S. Spector, Elina V. Kirichenko, and Ryan Gibson, *Russia, the US and the Missile Technology Control Regime* (London: IISS, Adelphi Paper 317, March 1998).

40. See Nikolai Novichkov, "Russia Details Illegal Deliveries to Armenia," *Jane's Defence Weekly*, April 16, 1997, p. 15; Glen E. Howard, "Oil and Missiles in the Caucasus," *The Wall Street Journal*, May 14, 1997, A22.

41. See David Hoffman, "Russian Missile Gyroscopes Were Sold to Iraq," *The Washington Post*, September 12, 1997, p. A33; and Vladimir Orlov and William C. Potter, "The Mystery of the Sunken Gyros," *Bulletin of the Atomic Scientists* (November–December 1998); 34–39.

42. Compare, for example, John Fialka, "U.S. Fears China's Success in Skimming Cream of Weapons Experts from Russia," *The Wall Street Journal*, October 14, 1993, A12, with "U.S. Opposes SS-18 Technology Sale to China," *The Washington Post*, May 22, 1996, A25; Stephen Blank, *The Dynamics of Russian Arms Sales to China* (Carlisle Barracks, PA.: Strategic Studies Institute, U.S. Army War College, 1997); and Joseph Kahn and Claudia Rosett, "China and Russia Rekindle Their Romance," *The Wall Street Journal*, April 24, 1996, A11.

43. See, for example, Ann Devroy and Daniel Williams, "Clinton: Reforms by Russia Outweigh Iran Reactor Deal," *The Washington Post*, April 14, 1995, A25.

44. See Robin Wright, "Russia Warned on Helping Iran Missile Program," *The Los Angeles Times*, February 12, 1997, A1, A6; Barbara Opal, "Israelis Say Russia Aids Iran's Quest for Missiles," *Defense News*, February 10–16, 1997, 1; Thomas Lippman, "U.S. Keeps after Russia to Halt Flow of Missile Technology to Iran,"

The Washington Post, January 18, 1998, A9; and Bill Gertz, "Russia Disregards Pledge to Curb Iran Missile Output," *The Washington Times*, May 22, 1997, A3.

45. See Yevgeniya Albats, *Novaya Gazeta Ponedelnik Russian No. 10*, "Hiring of Missile Experts for Iran Described," take 5 of 7, March 16–22, 1998.

46. For an excellent chronology of these events, see Stuard D. Goldman, Kenneth Katzman, Robert D. Shuey, and Carl E. Behrens, "Russian Missile Technology and Nuclear Reactor Transfers to Iran," *CRS Long Report for Congress 98–299* (Washington, D.C.: Congressional Research Service, 1998).

47. This legislation finally was made into law in the year 2000. See "Iran Nonproliferation Act of 2000," an amendment to H.R. 1883, printed in U.S. Congress, *Congressional Record*, February 22, 2000, p. S692.

48. See White House, Office of the Press Secretary, "Statement by the President," March 14, 2000; U.S. Congress, House, International Relations Committee, Press Release, "Iran Nonproliferation Act Passes House," March 1, 2000; and the praise of Senators Trent Lott and Joe Lieberman in Steven Mufson and Eric Pianin, "Senate Puts Condition on Space Station Aid," *The Washington Post*, February 25, 2000, A11.

49. Presidents Reagan and Bush also approved high technology dual-use exports to China as part of their cold war effort to build China up against the Soviet Union. For an unclassified tally of these U.S. exports, see Gary Milhollin, *U.S. Exports to China 1988–1998: Fueling Proliferation* (Washington, D.C.: Wisconsin Project on Nuclear Arms Control, April 1999).

50. John Landay, "US China Policy: The Sweet and Sour," *Christian Science Monitor*, March 18, 1996, p. 1; Milhollin, *U.S. Exports to China 1988–1998: Fueling Proliferation*.

51. See U.S. Congress, House, Select Committee on U.S. National Security and Military/Commercial Concerns with the Peoples Republic of China, *U.S. National Security and Military/Commercial Concerns with the Peoples Republic of China*, vol. I (Washington, D.C.: USGPO, May 1999), ii–xxiv.

52. On these points, see Randy J. Rydell, "Giving Nonproliferation Norms Teeth: Sanctions and the NPPA," *The Nonproliferation Review* (Winter 1999); 1–19.

53. See note 33, *Report of the Commission to Assess the Ballistic Missile Threat to the United States*, July 15, 1998, Pursuant to Public Law 201, 104th Congress.

54. See, for example, the recommendations of the Commission to Assess the Organization of the Federal Government to Combat the Proliferation of Weapons of Mass Destruction, in *Combating Proliferation of Weapons of Mass Destruction*, Pursuant to Public Law 293, 104th Congress, July 14, 1999, 76–79.

U.S. Ambassador Bernard Baruch (right) is pictured above with Jacob A. Malik, the Soviet delegate to the United Nations Disarmament Commission. One of the key issues that prompted the Soviets to reject the Baruch Plan was Ambassador Baruch's insistence that no single nation be able to veto UN Security Council actions against violators of international atomic energy controls. Courtesy of United Nations.

A key author of the Acheson-Lilienthal Report, which was the basis of the Baruch Plan, J. Robert Oppenheimer also authored the Report of the Panel of Consultants on Disarmament, which prompted Eisenhower's Atoms for Peace proposal. © Bettman/CORBIS.

U.S. President Dwight D. Eisenhower presenting his Atoms for Peace proposal before the UN, December 8, 1953. Courtesy of United Nations.

Concerned about the prospect of an accidental or catalytic war, which even the spread of one weapon to one additional nation might prompt, U.S. Ambassador James Wadsworth tried unsuccessfully to tighten International Atomic Energy Agency (IAEA) safeguards to prevent such proliferation. Courtesy of United Nations.

Irish Foreign Minister Frank Aiken (left) and his 1958 resolution concerning the spread of nuclear weapons prompted negotiation of the Nuclear Nonproliferation Treaty (NPT). Courtesy of United Nations.

U.S. Secretary of Defense Les Aspin announced the Counterproliferation Initiative December 7, 1993, and worked to institutionalize the initiative within the Department of Defense. Wally McNamee/CORBIS.

6
Counterproliferation

As the war with Iraq approached in early 1990, U.S. Defense Department officials noticed a shortcoming that had less to do with how well the NSG, MTCR, and AG were controlling exports than with what they were not controlling at all. Several smaller nations were attempting to acquire nuclear weapons and chemical and biological agents and the missiles to deliver them. But they also were acquiring computational, submersible, guidance, command, control, communication, and intelligence capabilities that would give them the kind of military advantages previously only attainable with weapons capable of mass destruction.

THE PROLIFERATION COUNTERMEASURES WORKING GROUP

This worried government security officials. One scenario they considered was that of Iran threatening to close the Strait of Hormuz not with nuclear weapons, but with submarine-launched homing torpedoes and advanced mines. Another scenario dealt with a replay of the war with Iraq. Defense Department officials worried that in the future, Iraq might threaten to close down an entire Saudi port not with chemical or biological weapons, but by targeting the port's ammunition and fuel stores with precise, slow flying conventional cruise missiles guided by satellite imagery, and satellite-assisted navigational services.

These same analysts were also concerned that with such discriminate military capabilities, smaller nations might be able to use nuclear, chemical, and biological munitions for strategic missions without killing large numbers of troops or civilians. Thus, North Korea might blind or disrupt U.S. and allied satellites, airborne warning systems, and ground-based military electronic systems by setting off a nuclear weapon in high space over the North Korean side of the demilitarized zone. Similarly, instead of using its massive chemical and biological arsenal to kill millions, North Korea might use relatively small amounts of agent to disrupt critical operations at essential U.S. and allied logistical and command centers.[1]

Certainly, the plausibility of such scenarios grew with the increasing availability of civilian technology of military significance. Such capabilities included satellite imagery; Global Positioning Satellite (GPS) and Global Navigational Satellite Systems (GLONASS) navigational signals; geographic information services; advanced computer hardware and software; encryption programs; mobile, secure communications systems; civilian space systems, and oceanographic and submersible technologies. In fact, the United States and other advanced nations were eager to sell such dual-use items. Trade in such items was profitable; foreign demand was high; and most of such commerce lay outside of the authority of existing proliferation control regimes.

In anticipation of these developments (and three months before Desert Shield), Secretary of Defense Dick Cheney created a directorate for Proliferation Countermeasures within the Office of the Deputy for Nonproliferation Policy.[2] Unlike the Counterproliferation Initiative, which was created four years later, this directorate had little to do with determining how the U.S. military might deter or pre-empt other nations' use of nuclear, chemical, or biological weapons militarily.[3] Rather, the directorate's first set of research projects (it commissioned over $2 million in studies annually) was focused on identifying which high-leverage conventional weapons systems might inflict strategic harm if effective military countermeasures were not developed.

To be sure, the directorate also worried about how best to limit the damage that nuclear, chemical, and biological weapons (and ballistic missiles carrying them) might do. Passive and active defenses (including missile defenses, protective gear, dispersion of forces, and offensive strikes once war began) were all studied.[4] But the directorate was under no illusion that truly effective military countermeasures were likely against such weapons. Steps could be taken to limit the damage they might do, but true countermeasures to neutralize them (as effectively as U.S. military electronic countermeasures were, for example, against Iraqi air defense radars) did not seem likely.[5]

Basing much of its work on research previously done in the Secretary of Defense's Office of Net Assessment, the Proliferation Countermeasures directorate, with Secretary Cheney's blessing, established a departmentwide Proliferation Countermeasures Working Group. This group included representatives from the Defense Intelligence Agency, the National Security Agency, the various military services, and the Joint Chiefs of Staff (JCS). The group's first project was to assess the threat that accurate Third World conventional ballistic missiles might present to U.S. expeditionary forces in the late 1990s.[6] This was followed by an examination of what military threats unmanned air vehicles (cruise missiles and reconnaissance remotely piloted vehicles) and improved civilian navigation, command, control, communication, and intelligence capabilities might pose to U.S. and allied forces.[7]

The aim of each of these studies was to anticipate possible proliferation threats well enough in advance to allow policy makers and military planners either to diffuse them or to deploy effective military countermeasures in a timely fashion. An additional goal was to try to refocus U.S. export control efforts on specific strategic dual-use technologies that posed the most immediate military threats.[8] There also was the hope that with the toughest problems, such anticipatory analysis might encourage these officials to develop more sophisticated, long-term country-specific strategies. These strategies, in turn, might pit American strengths against the natural or inherent weaknesses of the governments most inclined to use such strategic weaponry against the United States and its friends. In time, these hostile regimes, preoccupied with shoring up their weaknesses, might collapse or fade away.[9]

By 1992, the Proliferation Countermeasures directorate began to share its analyses both in the United States and overseas[10] and encouraged members of the Countermeasures Working Group to sponsor research of their own. The directorate's marginal success in engaging others on these high-technology issues, however, was soon overwhelmed by much stronger political and bureaucratic interests that emerged after America's war against Iraq. These forces made focusing on weapons capable of mass destruction priority number one.

FIRST THOUGHTS ON COUNTERPROLIFERATION

Desert Storm was won with precision guided munitions and advanced conventional weapons. Yet, its key effect was to heighten concern about the spread of crude missiles and nuclear, chemical, and biological weapons. The Soviet Union's collapse, meanwhile, had released hundreds of U.S. arms control and East-West export control officials from any pressing purposeful mission. Finally, there was the pressure of politics. Presidential elections in 1992 had Democrats emphasizing how lax U.S. export controls had been prior to Desert Storm. This set the stage for a Republican response.

Late in the summer of 1992, the Office of the Principal Deputy Under

Secretary of Defense for Strategy and Resources suggested ways to strengthen the Defense Department's efforts against strategic weapons proliferation. Under the reorganization proposed, a new deputy under secretary of defense would be created to oversee the activities of the Defense Trade Security Administration, the Office of the Deputy for Nonproliferation Policy, and the Deputy Assistant Secretary for Conventional Forces and Arms Control Policy (all together, approximately 200 people). Ironically, the suggested title for this deputy—Deputy Under Secretary for Counterproliferation—was originally considered for the director for Proliferation Countermeasures three years before but rejected because it was too vague. Did creating a deputy for counterproliferation mean that the Defense Department was going to neutralize weapons of mass destruction with advanced technology? Or was such "countering" to be accomplished with more traditional military counteroffensives or with counterintelligence? Did counterproliferation—whatever it was— include existing nonproliferation efforts or were these activities at odds with one another? In 1989, no one knew.

Yet, what seemed obscure in 1989, by 1992 seemed intriguing. Literally hundreds of draft view charts were composed explaining what counterproliferation might mean and what a deputy under secretary implementing it might do. Yet, none of these briefings were ever used. First, in September 1992, Deputy Secretary of Defense Donald Atwood thought better of reorganizing the department during the closing months of the presidential campaign and put a freeze on the creation of any new offices. Then, two months later, President Bush lost the election.

Clinton and the new officials he brought on were eager to reorganize the government, including the offices focused on proliferation issues. Several senior Clinton defense advisors had already considered what was needed while serving as members of the Defense Policy and Science Boards for the Bush administration. The Defense Science Board, in particular, had spent more than a year analyzing what new defensive and counteroffensive technologies might be developed to respond to other nations' threatened use of chemical, biological, and nuclear armed ballistic missiles. The board concluded that with enough advanced sensors, counteroffensive missile technologies, and intelligence, the U.S. military might be able to destroy the bulk of an enemy's offensive missiles before they ever left their launchers.

Two key Democratic board members—John Deutch, who later became under secretary for acquisition and, then, deputy secretary of defense in the Clinton administration, and Ashton Carter, who became assistant secretary of defense for nuclear security and counterproliferation— warmly embraced the board's findings. In an essay on intelligence requirements written for the Council on Foreign Relations prior to his appointment, Dr. Carter argued that combating the spread of weapons of

mass destruction with precision weapons required much more precise
and timely intelligence. What was most critical, he argued, was to know
when a nation was about to acquire one or two weapons and where
these weapons might be. It was one thing, he noted, to collect intelligence
on nations acquiring fissile material to make their first bomb but

planning an air strike on the nuclear facilities of a nation approaching construction of a first bomb, by contrast, requires entirely different types of collection
and analysis. Military planners need to study the building the raid is supposed
to destroy. The aircraft delivering the bombs will require information about the
location, radar frequencies and signal structures, and command and control of
air defenses surrounding the target. If cruise missiles and other "smart weapons"
are to be used, terrain contour maps, terminal area images, global positioning
coordinates, and other precision guidance information will have to be assembled.[11]

Although such planning would naturally be useful to limit damage once
a new nuclear nation went to war against the United States, Dr. Carter
emphasized, in a section entitled "Attacking a Fledgling Program or Arsenal," that it also would be particularly useful "in the event of an offensive U.S. attack."[12]

THE COUNTERPROLIFERATION INITIATIVE

Planning to fight proliferation and even to launch pre-emptive strikes
was new. More important, it resonated with the new secretary of defense,
Les Aspin, who as chairman of the House Armed Services Committee,
had argued that the spread of weapons of mass destruction was now
America's number one security concern. On December 7, 1993, after
months of briefings on what the Counterproliferation Initiative might
be, the secretary of defense announced the program before an audience
at the National Academy of Sciences.

Much of the speech was straightforward. In addition to working with
the State Department to try to prevent the proliferation of weapons of
mass destruction, Secretary Aspin called on the Defense Department to
work harder to protect against these weapons' possible use.[13] What
caught most people's attention, however, was the secretary's assertion
that providing such protection constituted a new, unique military mission and that he had formally directed the military services to "develop
new military capabilities to execute it."[14]

Although Aspin left the Pentagon right after announcing the Counterproliferation Initiative, he tried his best to institutionalize it. First, he
established a new post for Dr. Carter as assistant secretary for Nuclear
Security and Counterproliferation. Second, he instructed the military

services to identify research and acquisition programs that needed to be funded to accomplish the new counterproliferation mission. He also had his deputy, John Deutch, make counterproliferation a Defense Department acquisition priority. Finally, he saw to it that language was introduced in the National Defense Authorization Act for fiscal year 1994 requiring his successor to identify precisely what additional counterproliferation spending was needed.

Not surprisingly, the first half of 1994 was a busy one for the initiative's supporters. In addition to Dr. Carter's office and that of his deputy assistant secretary for counterproliferation, an additional deputy assistant secretaryship was created within the office of the under secretary of defense for acquisition. This new acquisition deputy was immediately put to work to answer Congress' reporting requirements concerning what new spending would be required to implement the Counterproliferation Initiative. In May, the Defense Department's reply was released, and Deputy Secretary Deutch asked the military services to find $400 million a year to fund fourteen "underfunded" counterproliferation programs that his acquisition staff had identified.[15]

The military services' reply was hardly enthusiastic. After months of review, the services earmarked no more than $80 million for possible use to fund programs supporting the counterproliferation mission. With this, the Office of the Secretary of Defense dropped any further talk of securing hundreds of millions of dollars for counterproliferation. Instead, Clinton's defense appointees now claimed that, in effect, the entire defense budget was in one way or another dedicated to counterproliferation. The office of the Joint Chiefs of Staff, meanwhile, contended that the counterproliferation "mission" was not a separate undertaking but rather one incorporated into all existing military missions.

Why was the military's initial support of the Counterproliferation Initiative so weak? Several Pentagon observers believe that the Clinton Pentagon had simply asked the military financially to sacrifice too much too soon.[16] In fact, while Deputy Secretary Deutch was asking the military to find $400 million in existing budget authority for counterproliferation, the White House was demanding significant cuts in overall defense spending. This undermined the secretary's credibility. In addition, the services resented having counterproliferation forced on them as a separate mission requirement with little or no consultation.[17] Certainly, the services could see the need to do more to prepare to fight in nuclear, chemical, and biological warfare environments. But such preparation was something they believed already had to be done as a part of existing military requirements to ensure command of sea, air, and land. Finally, some in the military were uneasy about the pre-emptive war tone of counterproliferation: What were the legal, moral, and operational ramifications of using U.S. military force prior to overt hostilities against proliferation targets that were practically impossible to find or to destroy entirely?[18]

In this regard, the military's concerns were amplified by the U.S. arms control community. They, too, suspected that the pre-emptive war aspect of the initiative was far more significant than publicly stated. They also were concerned that the Defense Department was abandoning its hard-line opposition to lax export controls, especially over dual-use items (e.g., computers and diagnostic equipment and other items useful for making strategic weapons). Counterproliferation was now what the Defense Department would do *after* export controls had failed to prevent proliferation: The Department's traditional use of military threat assessments to fortify other agencies' export control efforts no longer seemed to be a priority.[19]

Finally, the arms control supporters worried that nonproliferation as a goal was being challenged. On the one hand, counterproliferation's backers were arguing that with enough military effort (and spending), the United States could so mitigate the threats posed by weapons of mass destruction that the United States and its allies could prevail on the battlefield even if these weapons were used.[20] Yet, if this were so, existing nonproliferation taboos against these weapons' use, which the United States had always been eager to strengthen, would be undermined.

Then, there was the problem of deterrence. Lacking chemical or biological weapons, the U.S. military reserved the option of deterring these weapons' use (and of nuclear weapons as well) by threatening U.S. nuclear counterstrikes.[21] Yet, the more the Pentagon developed this option, the more arms control advocates worried that it would make other nations' acquisition of nuclear weapons seem justified. All of this and the initiative's feared flirtations with preventative war encouraged extensive debate.

DEFINING COUNTERPROLIFERATION BUREAUCRATICALLY

More important, the Counterproliferation Initiative prompted substantive and bureaucratic worries at the State Department, which had traditionally maintained control over proliferation issues. In the weeks following Secretary Aspin's announcement of the Counterproliferation Initiative, debates broke out between State and Defense officials and even within the Defense Department over what the initiative covered. Some officials wanted all proliferation concerns including advanced conventional weapons to be included; others did not. There also were disagreements over who was in control of counterproliferation policy. The State Department insisted that it should be in command of the initiative since it chaired the interagency working group on proliferation. The Defense

Department, meanwhile, was just as insistent that it have a free hand since the Counterproliferation Initiative was its idea, and it was footing most of the bill for the initiative's implementation. ACDA and the Department of Energy also had a stake in the matter, as did the intelligence agencies that were trying to budget and reorganize themselves to respond to new requirements.

By January 1994, the National Security Council staff was asked to resolve these issues. By mid-February, the council settled the key dispute between the State and Defense departments by brokering a set of definitions that both departments could accept but that favored the Department of State. Proliferation was defined descriptively: "The spread of nuclear, biological and chemical capabilities and the missiles to deliver them." Meanwhile, nonproliferation was defined as being Washington's comprehensive policy against proliferation, which employed the

full range of political, economic and military tools to prevent proliferation, reverse it diplomatically or protect our interests against an opponent armed with weapons of mass destruction or missiles, should that prove necessary. Nonproliferation tools include: intelligence, global nonproliferation norms and agreements, diplomacy, export controls, security assurances, defenses and the application of military force.[22]

This did not leave much for counterproliferation, which was reduced to the redundancy of being the "activities of the Department of Defense" to support nonproliferation "with particular responsibility for assuring that U.S. forces and interests can be protected should they confront an adversary armed with weapons of mass destruction or missiles."[23]

Although somewhat confusing, this definition had three clear advantages. First, by keeping nonproliferation as the comprehensive term to describe America's efforts against the spread of weapons of mass destruction, the policy focus was kept on the most horrible and indiscriminate weapons and on existing international and U.S. diplomatic nonproliferation efforts in general. As such, it gave the State Department ultimate control over any counterproliferation effort since, now, by definition, counterproliferation was subsumed under nonproliferation. Second, it avoided the vagueness inherent to any set of prescriptive definitions. A prescriptive definition might help clarify why weapons of mass destruction were of proliferation concern and what else might qualify and why. But such definitions were certain to generate the kind of debates over what should be included that the NSC definition memo was crafted to avoid. Finally, by limiting proliferation to weapons of mass destruction and the missiles to deliver them, the NSC definition kept conventional military systems and dual-use items that the United

States wanted to export to its friends out of the web of nonproliferation export controls.

The bureaucratic advantages that these definitions offered, however, came at a price. Certainly, as long as proliferation concerns were limited to weapons of mass destruction and ballistic missiles, any hope of developing truly effective military countermeasures (distinct from defenses and damage limiting measures) would necessarily remain distant. More important, the NSC definitions and their preoccupation with weapons of mass destruction kept counterproliferation from addressing the technical revolution in military affairs that even smaller nations were now engaged in. Thus, some of the most interesting of emerging strategic threats were placed beyond the initiative's reach. This was regrettable, since some of these new threats (particularly those posed by conventional cruise missiles, crude information warfare, and submersibles) were precisely the ones that were most amenable to the development of effective military countermeasures and targeted export controls.[24]

COUNTERPROLIFERATION IN OPERATION

Perhaps *because* of the military's initial weak reaction to the Counterproliferation Initiative,[25] the services' staffs did eventually begin to take more serious steps to evaluate the damage limitation requirements that nuclear, chemical, and biological weapons might impose against U.S. forces. Thus, in 1993, the Army, Navy, and Air Force staff created a Joint Program Office within the Department of Defense to address the shortcomings in U.S. preparations to fight adversaries that might use such weapons. This came after years of resistance to such ideas.

More important, the military finally began routine annual war games that focused on the effects nuclear, chemical, and biological weapons might have on U.S. forces.[26] A little over a year after Secretary Aspin's announcement of the Counterproliferation Initiative, the Navy incorporated nuclear, biological, and chemical weapons threats into their annual Naval War College war game, Nimble Dancer. Serious problems were encountered in playing out these games, but despite this, the Navy decided at the highest levels to continue to highlight chemical, biological, and nuclear weapons threats in follow-up war games.

Financially, however, the initiative enjoyed only mixed success. As noted before, Deputy Secretary of Defense John Deutch attempted in 1994 to increase government-wide funding for counterproliferation-relevant research and hardware acquisition by some $400 million annually. Yet, even the White House only requested $164 million to redress these. Moreover, the JCS earmarked only a third of the $230 million in Defense Department counterproliferation shortfalls Deutch had identified (the others were associated with the intelligence community and the

Department of Energy). Two years later, things had hardly improved. In fact, an internal Pentagon review in 1996 concluded that the department was still failing to fund some of the highest priority counterproliferation programs (e.g., biological agent detectors). Finally, in 1999, the department announced it would spend approximately $1 billion over the next five years to address these deficiencies.[27] Although the military has received protection against common anthrax infection, there was plenty of controversy over this and much more that had to be done.

As for the operational implementation of counterproliferation, the Defense Department initially did some planning and actually considered two offensive campaigns. First, late in 1993 the United States acted on intelligence that the Chinese were shipping chemical weapons-related materials to Iran. The White House considered interdicting the shipment but the suspect ship, the *Yin He*, turned out not to be carrying the illicit materials. Second, during the 1994 nuclear crisis with North Korea, the U.S. Air Force briefed Secretary of Defense William Perry on how it might bomb the North Korean nuclear reactor at Yongbyon. Given the high costs and uncertainties of this operation, the White House took a diplomatic approach instead.[28] In exchange for several billion dollars in oil and nuclear energy assistance, North Korea pledged not to operate its known nuclear facilities and eventually to allow inspections and to dismantle these facilities.[29]

The two largest counterproliferation operations that the services actually executed came four years later. In 1998, U.S. cruise missiles were fired against a suspected Sudanese chemical weapons plant and against Iraqi chemical, biological, and missile production plants. Neither campaign, however, was a clear success. Following the attack against the Sudan, evidence emerged that the plant U.S. missiles destroyed may have been a pharmaceutical facility, not a weapons factory.[30] As for Operation Desert Fox against Iraq, its effects were only temporary. As the commander-in-chief of U.S. Central Command, General Anthony Zinni, publicly noted, bombing Saddam Hussein's biological and chemical plants could hardly stop these programs, since making chemical and biological weapons was so easy.[31]

None of this helped the initiative bureaucratically. Unable to secure large sums for a new, separate counterproliferation mission, Department of Defense officials began arguing that nearly the entire defense budget was targeted against the threat of proliferation. Perhaps reflecting this sense of success, in 1996 the secretary of defense eliminated the post of assistant secretary for counterproliferation and the post of deputy assistant secretary of defense for counterproliferation. By 2000, all that remained within the office of the Secretary of Defense was a counterproliferation directorate. Its most public function was to coordinate proliferation-related meetings with NATO and other nations. The bulk of the initiative's acquisition activities, which focused on passive biological and chemical weapons defenses, though, continued.

By the year 2000 the initiative's emphasis clearly had shifted. Originally the initiative was animated by the prospect that offensive military operations might neutralize or roll-back the threat of strategic weapons proliferation. Seven years later, however, the initiative had been reduced to the less heroic but still critical concern of limiting whatever damage U.S. expeditionary forces might suffer if, as seemed likely, chemical, nuclear, or biological weapons were used against them. In short, the word *counterproliferation* had survived, but the hope that the initiative might neutralize the proliferation threats the United States and its allies faced had not.

NOTES

1. For an unclassified review of this research see Henry D. Sokolski, "Non-apocalyptic Proliferation: A New Strategic Threat?" *The Washington Quarterly* (Spring 1994): 115–27. Also see Andrew F. Krepinevich, "Cavalry to Computer: The Pattern of Military Revolutions," *The National Interest* (Fall 1994): 30–42; Patrick J. Garrity, "Implications of the Persian Gulf War for Regional Powers," *The Washington Quarterly* (Summer 1993): 153–170; and Thomas G. Mahnken, "America's Next War," *The Washington Quarterly* (Summer 1993): 171–84.

2. This directorate of Proliferation Countermeasures (PC) was created in April 1990 in the Office of the Deputy for Nonproliferation Policy (NPP). The deputy's office and the directorate under it reported to the assistant secretary of Defense for International Security Affairs and the under secretary of Defense for Policy.

3. In fact, one of the classified studies the directorate commissioned in 1991 was designed to gauge just how difficult and unlikely pre-emptive use of special forces against other nations' weapons of mass destruction would be.

4. The directorate's analyses were briefed to both the Central Command and the Marine Corps in the summer and fall of 1991. As a result, the Marine Corps conducted the first set of service war games on nuclear threats the following year.

5. Indeed, a key premise of getting the military to spell out just how harmful strategic weapons were against U.S. and coalition forces was to increase political pressures on other agencies of government to be more vigilant in restraining U.S. exports of strategic technology and to prioritize these efforts.

6. See Barbara Starr, "DoD to Track TBM Proliferation," and "Third World SSM Threat Studied," *Jane's Defence Weekly*, February 10, 1990, 226, and November 16, 1991, 944.

7. See Steve Wooley, "Proliferation of Precision Navigation Technologies and Security Implications for the U.S.," (Alexandria, VA: Institute for Defense Analyses, December 9, 1991); Berner and Lamphier and Associates, "Proliferation of Space Technology" (Bethesda, MD, Berner and Lamphier and Associates, October 18, 1991); and Matthew O'Brien, "C3I Upgrades for Developing Nations' Missile Operations" (Alexandria, VA: Institute for Defense Analyses, 1992). For an

unclassified review of this research, see Henry D. Sokolski, "Nonapocalyptic Proliferation: A New Strategic Threat?" *The Washington Quarterly* (Spring 1994): 115–27.

8. It was during this period, from 1990 through 1992, that the Defense Department pushed for and succeeded in making detailed dual-use item additions to the MTCR, the NSG, and the AG control lists.

9. This competitive strategies planning approach to proliferation was first briefed to the intelligence community in 1993. These briefings actually bore fruit. The intelligence community created a pilot program and later an actual office within the Central Intelligence Agency to hypothesize high-leverage advanced conventional arms threat scenarios and work backwards from them to develop new intelligence requirements and military and political strategies that might mitigate the threats. For an unclassified version of this brief, see Henry Sokolski, "Fighting Proliferation with Intelligence," *ORBIS* (Spring 1994): 245–60.

10. Secretary Cheney authorized Proliferation Threat Bilaterals to be held with the French Defense Ministry in 1991 and the British Defense Ministry the following year. Altogether, three bilaterals were held.

11. See Robert D. Blackwill and Ashton B. Carter, "The Role of Intelligence," in *New Nuclear Nations: Consequences for U.S. Policy*, edited by Robert D. Blackwill and Albert Carnesale (New York: Council on Foreign Relations Press, 1993), 234.

12. Ibid., 239–40.

13. See remarks by Honorable Les Aspin, Secretary of Defense, National Academy of Sciences, Committee on International Security and Arms Control, December 7, 1993, reprinted in Carnegie Endowment for International Peace, *The Counter-Proliferation Debate* (Washington, D.C.: Carnegie Endowment for International Peace, November 17, 1993).

14. Ibid., 4.

15. In addition to traditional passive defenses to limit damage, these programs included development of radars that might find underground command centers, systems that could acquire mobile SCUD missile launchers before they fired their missiles, and non-nuclear munitions that might interfere with an adversary's electronic command, control, and communications systems. See Office of the Deputy Secretary of Defense, Counterproliferation Review Committee, *Report on Activities and Programs for Countering Proliferation and NBC Terrorism* (Washington, D.C.: Counterproliferation Review Committee, May 1994), ES-2.

16. See, for example, Robert Holzer and Theresa Hitchens, "Pentagon Slows Counterproliferation Efforts," *Defense News*, August 29–September 4, 1994, 8.

17. After the Joint Chiefs of Staff rejected Deputy Secretary Deutch's plea for $400 million in June 1994, civil-military tensions over the program increased to the point where Assistant Secretary Carter declared that if the services "do not hear the music, then we will have to do it ourselves" (i.e., threaten to override JCS five-year budget planning). This threat was never carried out. See Barbara Starr, "The Jane's Interview: Ashton Carter," *Jane's Defence Weekly*, July 30, 1994, 40.

18. See, for example, Frank Gibson Goldman, *The International Legal Ramifications of United States Counter-Proliferation Strategy* (Newport, RI: Center for Naval Warfare Studies, April 1997). Such concerns, it should be noted, were generally not shared by Special Operations staffs.

19. For an overview of this debate, see Chris Williams, "DoD's Counterproliferation Initiative: A Critical Assessment," in *Fighting Proliferation: New Concerns for the Nineties*, edited by Henry Sokolski (Maxwell Air Force Base, AL: Air University Press, September 1996), 249–56. Also see Harold Muller and Mitchell Reiss, "Counterproliferation: Putting New Wine in Old Bottles," *The Washington Quarterly* (Spring 1995): 143–54; and Leonard S. Spector, "Neo-Nonproliferation," *Survival* (Spring 1995): 66–85. By the spring of 1994, Pentagon officials began reacting to such accusations defensively, publicly denying that the initiative had anything to do with pre-emption. See Thomas W. Lippman, "If Nonproliferation Fails, Pentagon Wants 'Counterproliferation' in Place," *The Washington Post*, May 15, 1994, A11.

20. See, for example, Office of the Secretary of Defense, *Proliferation: Threat and Response* (Washington, D.C.: USGPO, November 1997), iii; and Ashton Carter and Celeste Johnson, "Beyond the Counterproliferation Initiative to a Revolution in Counterproliferation Affairs," *National Security Studies Quarterly* (Summer 1999): 83–90.

21. See, for example, Center for Counterproliferation Research, *U.S. Nuclear Policy in the 21st Century* (Washington, D.C.: Center for Counterproliferation Research, National Defense University, 1998), 217–18, 240–43, and Barry R. Schneider, "Counterforce," in *Countering the Proliferation and Use of Weapons of Mass Destruction*, edited by Peter Hayes (New York: McGraw-Hill, 1998), 243–46.

22. Daniel Poneman, special assistant to the President and senior director for Nonproliferation and Export Controls, Memorandum for Robert Gallucci (Assistant Secretary for Political Military Affairs, Department of State) and Ashton Carter (Assistant Secretary for Nuclear Security and Counterproliferation, Department of Defense), "Agreed Definitions," February 18, 1994, available from author upon request.

23. Ibid.

24. Trade controls, again, might not stop commerce in critical dual-use technologies but might slow it long enough to allow the development and employment of effective military countermeasures to new threats before these threats are fully realized. For a detailed unclassified description of how the Pentagon used this approach to cope with Iraq's possible employment of the Condor II, an advanced conventional ballistic missile, see Henry Sokolski, "The Military Implications of Proliferation in the Middle East," Testimony before a hearing of the Senate Subcommittee on Technology and National Security of the Joint Economic Committee (Washington, DC, USGPO, March 13, 1992), p. 112, "Arms Trade & Nonproliferation in the Middle East, Part II."

25. In fact, in interviews, at least two senior Defense Department officials privately noted that the initiative's rash implementation caused so much unnecessary dissension between OSD and the services that it initially set *back* military preparedness efforts against nuclear, biological, and chemical threats between one and two years.

26. As already noted, the Bush Pentagon tried to get such games started. In April 1992, the Marine Corps War Gaming and Assessment Center at Quantico conducted what it hoped would be the first of a series of such war games. After reviewing the results, which were disturbing, the Marine Corps canceled plans for follow-up games.

27. See Thomas Mahnken, "A Critical Appraisal of the Defense Counterproliferation Initiative," *National Security Studies Quarterly* (Summer 1999): 91–102.

28. Don Oberdorfer, *The Two Koreas: A Contemporary History* (Reading, MA: Addison-Wesley, 1997), 323.

29. This understanding, known as the 1994 Agreed Framework, can be found along with an official explanation and a critique by experts outside of government in Henry Sokolski, *Fighting Proliferation: New Concerns for the 1990s* (Maxwell Air Force Base, AL: Air University Press, 1996), 183–212, 309–318.

30. See "Was the Sudan Raid on Target?" MSNBC, December 29, 1999, http://www.msnbc.com/news/331435.asp?cp1=1; James Risen, "To Bomb Sudan Plant, Or Not: A Year Later, Debates Rankle," *New York Times*, October 27, 1999, A1; Oriana Zil, "The Controversial U.S. Retaliatory Missile Strikes," *Frontline/New York Times* Special Report, April 13, 1999; Frontline, 1999http://www.pbs.org/wgbh/pages/frontline/shows/binladen/bombings/retaliation.html; Tim Weiner and James Risen, "Decision to Strike Factory in Sudan Based Partly on Surmise," *New York Times*, September 21, 1998; and Michael Barletta, "Chemical Weapons in the Sudan: Allegations and Evidence," *The Nonproliferation Review* 6, no. 1 (1998): 115–36.

31. See William M. Arkin, "Desert Fox Delivery: Precision Undermined its Purpose," *The Washington Post*, January 17, 1999, B1.

7

The Next Campaign

In considering the next campaign against proliferation, it is tempting to work free from the shadow of history. Indeed, as Americans, we prefer working with a clean slate. Yet, doing so with proliferation threats would be a mistake. First, the history of nonproliferation can give us a better understanding of what we are doing today. Second, the specific strengths and weaknesses of past efforts against proliferation suggest what we should do in the future. Finally, these programs' penchant for relying on questionable or transitory strategic insights highlights what any future campaign against proliferation would do well to avoid.

PAST AS PRESENT

An example of where current U.S. nonproliferation policy can be better understood using the lens of history is the 1994 Agreed Framework that the United States reached with North Korea. When this deal was first announced, several experts compared it to the Kennedy-Khrushchev understandings reached during the Cuban missile crisis of 1962.[1] Yet, this historical reference offers far less insight into the agreement than does the history of Articles IV, VI, and X of the NPT. The 1994 crisis came, after all, not because North Korea was threatening to bomb the United States, but because Pyongyang decided to exercise its rights under the NPT. More important, North Korea's actions in 1994 were shaped by its understanding of the NPT.

Like Italy and others in the early 1960s, who demanded that the NPT allow members the freedom to leave the treaty if their supreme national interests were jeopardized, North Korea wanted out in 1994. Pyongyang joined the NPT in 1985 at Russia's urging after it was discovered North Korea was building an unsafeguarded reactor optimized for plutonium production. To get Pyongyang to join, Moscow and the IAEA promised to build several light water reactors, none of which North Korea ever received.[2] As Pyongyang saw it, then, Western demands in the early 1990s for NPT-based inspections were all stick and no carrot: They not only jeopardized North Korea's sovereign right to develop nuclear power to provide electricity, but ignored U.S.–South Korean military exercises, which left North Korea defenseless against nuclear intimidation.[3] In addition, North Korea insisted that the NPT recognize its right to produce weapons-usable plutonium so long as Pyongyang could claim (as Japan had) that the material would be used for "peaceful purposes." Giving up its NPT rights to produce such materials, as North Korea agreed to do only made sense if it was compensated (as Article IV of the NPT encouraged) with other new nuclear technology. In specific, the United States agreed that North Korea should receive a set of much larger, modern light water reactors of U.S. design similar to those that both Moscow and the IAEA had failed to supply previously.[4]

As for the U.S. military threat assessments of North Korea that helped prompt the deal, these too make more sense when viewed from the perspective of the NPT. In specific, they reflected the finite deterrence assumptions underlying Articles IV, V, VI, and X of the NPT. Pyongyang might acquire a few nuclear weapons, according to the chairman of the Joint Chiefs of Staff, but this would hardly constitute much of a threat to the United States. Only when North Korea acquired many weapons, the chairman argued, would Pyongyang have a force that could destroy enough key airfields and ports in South Korea to produce a militarily significant result. A smaller crude arsenal of only one or two weapons, on the other hand, was far less of a worry. All it could be used for is to target a major allied city—a threat that America's much larger force could easily deter.[5]

Viewed through the NPT assumptions of 1968, then, the 1994 Agreed Framework made perfect sense. A question worth asking, however, is just how sound these assumptions are today. Is finite deterrence a sound way to assess the North Korean nuclear threat? Even if Washington could deter North Korea from striking the United States or its Asian allies with nuclear weapons and missiles, wouldn't Pyongyang still be able to use these systems to intimidate Japan, a nation whose bases are essential for U.S. conventional forces to defend Seoul? What of North

Korea's ability to threaten America with a nuclear strike? Might this deter the United States from executing its declared strategy of striking deep with conventional forces against Pyongyang if the north attacked the south? Then there is the question of how sound Washington and Pyongyang's interpretation is of the NPT. Can the NPT ever prevent North Korean proliferation if the treaty is viewed as guaranteeing Pyongyang the right to come within days of having nuclear explosives and encourages nuclear powers to give it the technology to do so even though nuclear power is currently impractical and uneconomical for Pyongyang?[6] These questions more than suggest that the Agreed Framework is no sounder than the NPT's key premises were in 1968.

This same point, in a different way can be made about current U.S. policy toward Iraq and Iran and the Baruch Plan. U.S. policy towards Iran and Iraq assumes as Baruch did that international inspections of these nations' nationally run nuclear activities are prone to fail; that the inspectors will only gain a false sense of confidence, while the inspected evade whatever safeguards are imposed.

Hence, the three alternative approaches the United States has taken towards Iran and Iraq. The first, and most preferred, is to establish total UN control of these countries' nuclear activities (as the Baruch Plan recommended and was arguably attempted with the UN Special Commission in Iraq). The second best (and the course now being pursued) is to try to deny these nations access to any potentially sensitive nuclear technology whether it is subject to IAEA inspections or not. Third, but least preferable, is to take military action against these nations if they are unwilling to end their nuclear programs (as the Acheson-Lilienthal Report called for and the United States has attempted in the case of Iraq).

However sound these views and approaches may be in theory, they have hardly been very sucessful when applied in the cases of Iran and Iraq. This ought not to be surprising. A more difficult point is the awkwardness of trying to apply absolute, Acheson-Lilienthal–like solutions to either Iran or Iraq. Again, what was questionable in 1946 is no less so today. Indeed, total international control over nuclear activities and support for military action against violators were two proposals the Soviets rejected in 1946 and that the United States and others today still have failed to get Iraq or Iran to accept.

Certainly, with nuclear technology so much more accessible than it was in the 1940s, trying to establish absolute controls over other nations' national nuclear programs today is problematic. Even in Iran's case, U.S. objections to the Russians finishing a partially completed German reactor at Bushehr are rebuttable. In fact, Iran is paying a cash-strapped Russia $800 million to bring one gigawatt of electricity on line. Although a natural gas-fired plant might be cheaper and more reliable once installed, it is unclear if the gas necessary to run it could be transported at an affordable price to the location of the planned plant or if those producing gas in Iran would be willing to sell the fuel for this purpose. These reactors, moreover, will be inspected by the IAEA and their plutonium-laden spent fuel may be removed to Russia. How much success is one likely to have trying to oppose such a deal? So far (besides efforts to block dangerous Russian exports of uranium enrichment plants and plutonium production reactors to Iran), the United States has had little.[7]

As for the even tighter controls and military actions the United States has taken against Iraq, these too have been less than totally successful. Indeed, only when the political regimes in Iran and Iraq give way is it likely that the proliferation threat in the Persian Gulf will abate. Just as Stalin and his style of rule had to die before there could be significant nuclear threat reductions between the superpowers, so, too, it is with the revolutionary regimes in Tehran and Baghdad.[8]

FORWARD FROM THE PAST

Besides giving us a deeper understanding of how sound current policy is, past nonproliferation efforts speak to what nonproliferation initiatives should aspire to in the future. In the case of the Baruch Plan, its exaggerated view of nuclear war and of the inability to deter or defend against nuclear aggression encouraged rather extreme recommendations about international control. That said, the plan was quite right in emphasizing the need to distinguish between safe and dangerous activities and materials. Safe activities and materials can be inspected or monitored with a high probability that any attempted military diversion will be detected before the diversion is complete and early enough to allow outside states the opportunity to intervene to stop it.

This timely warning criteria is difficult to meet. But it is critical to having effective safeguards whether one has absolute international controls, like the Baruch Plan envisioned, or merely occasional inspections of nationally run programs as the IAEA and the Chemical Weapons Convention's inspectorate (the Organization for the Prohibition of Chemical Weapons) currently conduct. As the Acheson-Lilienthal Report made clear, weapons-usable fuels (such as highly enriched uranium and separated plutonium and thorium) and the facilities where these materials are produced or used in bulk (plutonium reprocessing plants, uranium enrichment facilities, fuel fabrication plants, reactors that use such fuels) cannot be safeguarded. Again, the reason why is simple: By the time a military diversion of these materials or activities could be detected there would be too little time to intervene to prevent a bomb from being made.

Any future campaign against strategic weapons proliferation would do well to assume as tough a criteria especially when speaking about safeguards for space launch, biological, chemical, and information technologies. Certainly, activities and equipment related to these technologies can be monitored. It is doubtful, though, if the criteria of timely warning could ever be achieved. Space launch vehicles, after all, are interchangeable with intermediate and intercontinental-range ballistic missiles. Chemical and biological facilities, meanwhile, can be shifted from peaceful to military production overnight and computers in a matter of seconds or less.

This suggests two things. First, there are limits to what can be safeguarded. Second, and because of this, far more thought needs to be given to what can safely be exported. One can share the benefits of peaceful satellites, for example, without sharing rocket technology. All that is needed is access to satellite services planned or already in place. Similarly, there is a surplus of high-end computational capabilities that can be easily accessed via the Internet. On the other hand, when the technology or materials in question cannot be safeguarded (as with advanced computers, space launch vehicles, and satellite-related launch integration information), nations should understand that if they export such goods, they may well be diverted to military purposes even if their use is monitored.

Certainly, this last point was one Atoms for Peace did not adequately consider and the consequences were calamitous. To be sure, had Eisenhower not pushed his program, nuclear proliferation would have occurred. Yet, without his program, this proliferation would have been far more limited and would have come much later. Because of this, it is tempting to dismiss Atoms for Peace and its global promotion of plutonium-producing power plants as "one of the most inexplicable political fantasies in history."[9] But to do so would be a mistake. Atoms for Peace may have gotten the relationship between vertical and horizontal proliferation wrong, but it at least recognized that there was a connection, and it was right to try to draw it. Of course, getting such matters correct is critical. Here, the program failed miserably.

That said, any serious future campaign against proliferation will have to try again to get such matters right. The reason why is simple: Global stockpiles of surplus nuclear weapons-usable materials are large and growing. This is not so much because nations are building more nuclear weapons, but because they are dismantling them and extracting several hundreds of bombs' worth of additional plutonium from spent civilian reactor fuel each year. These surplus stockpiles' growth is relatively new. In 1986, at the height of the cold war, virtually all the world's nuclear weapons material was locked up in over 69,000 deployed U.S., British,

French, Russian, and Chinese nuclear warheads. With the exception of the Chinese, all of these countries have since reduced their nuclear deployments dramatically. U.S. deployments have fallen from a high of over 32,000 weapons to approximately 7,000. Russia's deployed arsenal declined dramatically as well from a high of 45,000 or more to approximately 6,000 strategic warheads and an additional number of tactical warheads.[10]

Although these deployment reductions are welcome, they are producing another set of challenges as the amount of surplus weapons-usable material grows. Although there is good information about the status, location, and numbers of surplus Western weapons-usable materials, there is not for Russia or China. The precise number of tactical weapons the Russians have deployed along with the number of inactive and ready reserve nuclear warheads they have on hand, for example, is unknown. Some experts believe that together, these numbers might exceed as many as 14,000 warheads. Then, there is the issue of surplus weapons-usable materials (separated plutonium and highly enriched uranium) that could be refashioned into bombs. Here, the uncertainties are no less dramatic, ranging from between 700 and 1,200 tonnes of highly enriched uranium and 135 and 150 tonnes of separated plutonium. The difference between the high and low numbers here is quite significant, being equivalent to over 23,000 advanced nuclear warheads.[11]

Compounding this growing and uncertain overhang of Russian military materials, are the large and expanding stockpiles of weapons-usable plutonium extracted from civilian spent fuel in Japan, India, Russia, and Western Europe. Although exact figures are unavailable, the best current estimates indicate that world civilian inventories contain at least 32,000 crude weapons worth of separated civilian plutonium.[12] These figures are large. Indeed, unless these surplus stockpiles (and the uncertainties surrounding them) stop growing and become less accessible, the risks of their theft or illicit transfer will only grow as the ability to account for and control these assets declines. Still, the world's strategic weapons states will have to reduce their reliance on such weaponry if they are to maintain the support of other nations against proliferation. The trick here will be to reduce existing strategic weapons inventories *without* increasing the world's access to ever larger and more uncertain amounts of strategic materials and capabilities.[13] In this, Atoms for Peace clearly did a poor job. But we should not assume that we are certain to do much better. In fact, current U.S. policy is to encourage international adoption of a military fissile material production cut-off treaty (FMCT), the essentials of which were first proposed in 1956 as a part of the Atoms for Peace Program. Not surprisingly, this proposal, like its Atoms for Peace predecessor, could actually facilitate an increase in weapons-usable material stockpiles by allowing continued production of highly enriched uranium and separated plutonium for civilian purposes.[14]

Clearly, we must do better. Success in reducing these surplus materials safely, however, will depend heavily on what we believe the relationship between horizontal and vertical proliferation is. Currently, there are two views—one sound and another quite frightening—both of which are rooted in the NPT. It matters considerably which one we choose. The first of these views reflects the thinking of the Irish resolutions of 1958. According to this outlook, the further spread of strategic weapons complicates reducing existing arsenals and makes cataclysmic wars more likely. As such, both weapons and nonweapons states have an equal stake in reducing horizontal proliferation.

The second view, as previously explained, reflects the finite deterrence thinking predominate at the NPT's signing in 1968. According to this view, each nation has a right to acquire nuclear weapons and is entitled to certain incentives, that is, access to all forms of civilian nuclear technology and progress toward the disarming of existing strategic arsenals, as *quid pro quos* for not exercising it. Progress in disarming, moreover, is defined in terms of Mutual Assured Destruction (MAD)-inspired arms control. The superpowers must agree to a comprehensive nuclear test ban (CTBT), limitations on first-strike capable strategic delivery systems (SALT and START), and to forswear national missile defenses (ABM). The hope here is to get the superpowers to reverse their strategic arms build-up by encouraging them to rely on slower, smaller, cruder forces that can only target cities. Innovation, stockpile augmentation, defense-offense competitions are bad; finite deterrence, mutual assured destruction, targeting civilians are good.

This second view, which senior Clinton officials have argued is "the foundation of our efforts to prevent proliferation of all . . . weapons of mass destruction,"[15] is rooted in the arms rivalry of the cold war. Yet, there is no longer a prospect of a global nuclear war between the West and the Warsaw Pact. Instead, what threatens peace are potential undeterrable wars that could be ignited with strategic weapons in North Africa, the Middle East, Southwest Asia, and the Far East or be set off by accidental attacks from existing nuclear weapons states.

In this world, the last way to promote nonproliferation would be to push an arms control agenda that presumes that using crude arsenals to threaten the destruction of cities is stabilizing and that defending against such attacks is dangerous. Nor, given what we now know about the costs and risks of nuclear power and space launch systems, should nonproliferation be tied to presumed "rights" to such technology. Certainly, attempts to demand such NPT-like rights to chemical and biological technology should raise flags.[16] Indeed, such NPT agendas are only likely to *encourage* more nations to acquire strategic weapons capabilities. At a minimum, any future effort against proliferation would want to reinterpret existing understandings, such as the NPT, by reference to the logic of the original Irish resolutions of 1958 rather than to MAD.[17]

Emphasizing this sounder strategic outlook should help. Yet, even without MAD-inspired nonproliferation, there will be a need for continued nonproliferation export controls. Certainly, the original assumptions behind such controls—that smaller nations' acquisition of strategic weapons would risk wider wars and undermine the influence and security of the United States and its allies—remain sound today. The problem now, however, is that without a global polarizing contest like the cold war, securing international adherence to such restraints is far more difficult and, if not approached properly, can be self-defeating. As became evident after Desert Storm, U.S. efforts to expand participation in the AG, NSG, and MTCR not only debased these regimes' membership, but encouraged technology transfers to entities clearly known to be proliferating.

This recommends both caution and modesty. It certainly is untenable for the United States to negotiate high levels of restraint and consensus as was done at the height of the cold war. Instead, the United States should promote restraints designed to work even though key supplier nations are likely to disagree about what should be controlled and to whom. One approach, now being tried, is to encourage other nations to adopt the kind of "catch all" controls the United States (and, recently, the European Union) adopted after Desert Shield and combine them with the no undercut provisions present in the NSG, AG, and MTCR. Under this scheme, members of existing control regimes would not have to reach agreement over particular lists of control items or destinations. Instead, each could deny any export (listed or not) to any destination and expect this denial to be upheld (i.e., not undercut) by the other members until they met to learn why the denial was made. This market-like case-by-case approach would encourage each member of these control regimes to persuade others of what should be controlled to whom. Over time, incremental agreement might be reached on a substantial number of items and destinations.[18]

As for sanctions and enforcement of these controls, international support is likely to be thin. Still, each nation, including the United States, has a strong interest in at least not subsidizing foreign entities that are known to be proliferating. Meeting this lower standard of restraint by prohibiting such support in national domestic laws certainly would not be as heroic as trying to sanction all misbehavior internationally. But such laws are more likely to be enforced and would, in fact, do more to curb proliferation than is currently the case.[19]

As for using the ultimate enforcement sanction of military action, the fate of the Counterproliferation Initiative suggests just how difficult and unlikely such actions will be. Limiting the damage strategic weapons might inflict on United States and allied forces and territory *after* they have proliferated through air, missile, chemical, and biological defenses, will (and should) enjoy support. These defenses, however, will hardly eliminate the strategic weapons threat. Offensive pre-emptive and pre-ventative strikes to *prevent* their proliferation, moreover, are unlikely ever to be mounted.

TOWARD A NONMILITARY CAMPAIGN

Of course, more than a few have already faulted the Counterprolifer-ation Initiative on this point. Yet, at a deeper level, the shortcomings of the Counterproliferation Initiative are shared by previous nonprolifera-tion efforts as well. As noted in the previous chapter, the U.S. Defense Department's first attempts to examine possible military countermea-sures against proliferation focused less on nuclear, chemical, and biolog-ical weapons, than on other advanced technologies. Although this effort was short-lived, any future campaign against proliferation will have to refocus on these threats. In fact, advanced simulations, maneuver war-fare, microelectro-mechanical systems, information warfare, munitions based on new physical principles, electromagnetic propulsion, advanced biotechnology, battle management, sensors, and new military operational doctrines are all likely to produce a revolution in military affairs of stra-tegic proportions.[20]

On the other hand, we still do not know precisely what shape this military revolution will take or what we should do to shape it. One, of course, could fault the Counterproliferation Initiative for not getting the right answers to these questions or for failing to focus on how the an-swers might impact on the likely use or development of weapons capable of mass destruction. But to do so would be a mistake. First, not many answers are yet available. Second, even if there were, it is doubtful that any nonproliferation effort based on them would be very sound.

In fact, every major nonproliferation effort to date has been based on one or another such strategic assessment. Yet, to varying degrees, these assessments were unsound or the strategic context the efforts assumed would prevail changed. To the extent that the dangers they focused on never existed or disappeared, their recommended policy solutions were also less than effective. Certainly, given past shortcomings in anticipating the implications or duration of strategic trends, there is little reason to believe that we will now suddenly get it entirely right.

This suggests the need to anchor the next campaign against proliferation in something more certain and lasting than technological or military insights alone. Fortunately, such trends exist. The best of them, in fact, promise growth in real wealth, liberal democratization, and pacification for an increasing number of nations. Real incomes for the nonrich countries of the world (those with per capita incomes below $8,000) have been on the rise, doubling from 1960 to 1990. They are prone to grow at least 2 percent per year, ensuring at least another doubling of real income within the next thirty-six years. Meanwhile, with the demise of the Soviet Union, socialism has receded as an ideological force supporting the most counterproductive forms of state economic interference (unproductive nationalization of industries, barriers to foreign capital investment and technology imports, damaging price, market, and employment controls, etc.). The net result has been not only real growth in the less developed world, but relative growth that finally is beginning to close the gap between the world's wealthy and nonrich nations.[21]

With this increased wealth has come improved levels of education and health and, most important, a net increase in the number of democracies. In fact, since the mid-1970s, the number of democracies (as defined by Freedom House assessments) has doubled from approximately thirty to sixty worldwide. Several analysts have noted that the correlation between per capita income growth and democratization is quite strong and have projected that at least another fifteen nations will become free in the next thirty years. These same writers also emphasize that democracies have shown either no or at least a very low propensity to engage in conflict with one another.[22]

The expansion of these "zones of peace" over those of "turmoil," then, is a trend that could obviate current concerns about strategic weapons proliferation. A world of Canadas is a world not at war. However, even the optimists among the analysts note that there are clear exceptions to this liberalizing trend. Several Arab-Islamic nations (even when the oil-rich ones are excluded) have gotten richer, more educated, and healthier *without* becoming more democratic. There also are serious debates among the experts over the middle and long-term political futures of China and Russia. These exceptions are hardly trivial: From a proliferation standpoint, they include the most serious threats.[23] Finally, unless a democratic government fully informs its public and allows debate over the merits of deploying new strategic weaponry, there is no assurance that the right decision will be made.[24]

Still, the progressive trend towards global democratization is a powerful engine for peace and suggests a new order of battle for nonproliferation. The challenge facing nonproliferation policy makers today, is, at a minimum, to contain the proliferation threats in the zones of turmoil. Indeed, focusing on this nonproliferation objective may be the surest way to get existing weapons states to reduce or eliminate their strategic weapons arsenals. Certainly, the contradictions within this zone's remaining illiberal regimes might play themselves out as favorably as they did in the Soviet Union's case and strategic wars will be avoided. On the other hand, this might not happen or it might take decades to occur. As with the fall of the Soviet Union, a favorable outcome is unlikely to arrive merely by chance. Indeed, the Soviets' decline was due in no small part to America's willingness to pit its relative military, political, and economic strengths against Moscow's relative weaknesses. The United States avoided war but was more than willing to compete against the Soviets by building up its military, restricting Soviet access to high technology, and demanding that Moscow respect human rights. This leveraged competition served to catalyze Moscow's political and economic contradictions and deficiencies and, over time, forced it to give way to a less threatening regime.[25]

What this suggests is that the next campaign would do well to explicitly distinguish between progressive and hostile illiberal regimes, something no previous nonproliferation initiative has yet done. More important, the next campaign should work in a fashion that actually promotes progressive over illiberal rule. For the United States and its allies, this should come naturally. Indeed, over the last decade, American and allied presidents have endorsed the idea that expanding the number of democratic nations is critical to international security. What is required now is to make U.S. and allied nonproliferation policy an integral part of this larger undertaking. Assuming it can be done, the results could be significant. Indeed, it could help ensure that the next campaign is the last.

NOTES

1. See, for example, Editorial, "Two Crises," *The Boston Globe*, December 23, 1994, 18; William Goldcamp, "Dealing Recklessly with North Korea," *The Washington Times*, April 10, 1995, A17; Charles Maynes, "Despite Establishment's Dismay Carter Displays Diplomatic Prowess," *The Los Angeles Times*, December 25, 1994, M2; and Terry Atlas, "Ability to 'Psych Out' Foes Crucial in Foreign Crisis," *Chicago Tribune*, October 23, 1994, sec. 4, 4.

2. On these points, see Marcus Noland, *Avoiding the Apocalypse: The Future of the Two Koreas* (Washington, D.C.: Institute for International Economics, June 2000), 146.

3. On North Korea's claim that U.S.–South Korean *Team Spirit* joint military exercises planned for 1993 constituted a nuclear threat that warranted its withdrawal from the NPT and its objections to IAEA special inspections, see Charles Downs, *Over the Line: North Korea's Negotiating Strategy* (Washington, D.C.: AEI Press, 1999), 220–25.

4. On these points, see the analysis of the Clinton administration's under sec-

retary of defense for policy, Walter Slocombe, "Resolution of the North Korean Nuclear Crisis," in *Fighting Proliferation: New Concerns for the 1990s*, edited by Henry Sokolski (Maxwell Air Force Base, AL: Air University Press, 1996), 187–89.

5. See press conference transcript, General John Shalakashvili, Department of Defense, Public Affairs, December 14, 1993, cited by Victor Gilinsky, *Nuclear Blackmail: The 1994 U.S.-Democratic People's Republic of Korea Agreed Framework on North Korea's Nuclear Program* (Stanford, CA: Hoover Institution, 1997), 8–9.

6. See Noland, *Avoiding the Apocalypse*, 343–44, 370–71; and David Albright and Kevin O'Neill, eds., *Solving the North Korean Nuclear Puzzle* (Washington, DC: Institute for Science and International Security, 2000), 42–55, 127–37, 187–97, 229–43.

7. On these points, see David A. Schearzbach, *Iran's Nuclear Program: Energy or Weapons?* (Washington, D.C.: Natural Resources Defense Council, 1995); Stuart D. Goldman, Kenneth Katzman, Robert D. Shuey, and Carl E. Behrens, "Russian Missile Technology and Nuclear Reactor Transfers to Iran," *CRS Long Report for Congress 98–299* (Washington, D.C.: Congressional Research Service, 1998); Mark Hibbs, "Iran May Keep Russian Spent Fuel or Take Plutonium, REPU, and Waste," *Nuclear Fuel*, December 18, 1995, 1.

8. On this point, see Daniel Byman, "A Farewell to Arms Inspections," *Foreign Affairs* (January/February 2000): 119–32; and Kenneth Timmerman, "Fighting Proliferation Through Democracy: A Competitive Strategies Approach Toward Iran," in *Prevailing in a Well-Armed World*, edited by Henry Sokolski (Carlisle, PA: Strategic Studies Institute, April 2000), 111–32.

9. See Leonard Beaton, *Must the Bomb Spread?* (Middlesex, UK: Penguin Books, 1966), 87–88. For similar views, also see George Quester, *Nuclear Diplomacy* (New York: The Dunellen Company, 1970), 99–100; Amory Lovins, *Soft Energy Paths: Toward a Durable Peace* (New York: Harper & Row, 1979), 205; J. G. Phillips, "Energy Report: Safeguards, Recycling Broadens Nuclear Power Debate," *National Journal Reports*, May 22, 1975, 421; and Harold Nieburg, *Nuclear Secrecy and Foreign Policy* (Washington, D.C.: Public Affairs Press, 1964), 19.

10. These deployment figures are expected to drop by at least another 50 percent over the next few years. See Steve Fetter, "A Comprehensive Transparency Regime for Warheads and Fissile Materials," *Arms Control Today* (January/February 1999): 4; and William M. Arkin and Robert S. Norris, "Global Nuclear Stockpiles, 1945–2000," "Russian Strategic Nuclear Forces," and "U.S. Nuclear Forces, 2000," *Bulletin of the Atomic Scientists* (March/April 2000), 79; (March/April 1998): 70–71; and (May/June 2000): 70.

11. For background analysis, see Henry Sokolski, "What Post-Cold War Proliferation Controls Require," testimony given before a hearing of the Senate Governmental Affairs Committee, April 12, 2000, available on the Web at www.wizard.net/~npec.

12. These figures are conservative and are drawn from David M. Albright and Lauren Barbour, *Plutonium Watch: Separated Plutonium Inventories Continue to Grow* (Washington, D.C.: ISIS Press, 1999); David Albright, *Separated Civil Plutonium Inventories: Current and Future Directions* (Washington, D.C.: ISIS Press, 2000); and David Albright, Frans Berkhout, and William Walker, *Plutonium and Highly Enriched Uranium 1996: World Inventories, Capabilities and Policies* (Oxford:

University Press, 1997). For much higher plutonium figures, see Robert S. Norris and William M. Arkin, "World Plutonium Inventories," *Bulletin of the Atomic Scientists* (September/October 1999): 71.

13. For a useful introduction to the relevant issues here, see Brian G. Chow et al., *A Concept for Strategic Materials Accelerated Removal Talks (SMART)* (Santa Monica, CA: RAND DRU-1338-DoE, April 1996).

14. For the case for a military fissile production cut-off treaty and the treaty's potential pitfalls, see David Albright and Kevin O'Neill, eds., *The Challenges of Fissile Material Control* (Washington, D.C.: The Institute for Science and International Security, 1999), and Brian G. Chow, Richard H. Speier, and Gregory S. Jones, *The Proposed Fissile-Material Production Cutoff: Next Steps* (Santa Monica, CA: RAND, MR-586-OSD, 1995).

15. For the connection White House officials see between the NPT, the CWC, the BWC, and the MTCR, see Anthony Lake, "A Year of Decisions: Arms Control and Nonproliferation in 1995," *The Nonproliferation Review* (Winter 1995): 55–59.

16. The language of Articles IV and III of the NPT is adapted virtually word for word in Article XI of the CWC. Article XI of the CWC is entitled "Economic and Technological Development." Provision 1 reads, "The Provisions of this Convention shall be implemented in a manner which avoids hampering the economic or technological development of States Parties and international cooperation in the field of chemical activities." Provision 2 (b) requires that States Parties shall "undertake to facilitate, and have the right to participate in the fullest possible exchange of chemical, equipment and scientific and technical information relating to the development and application of chemistry for purposes not prohibited under this Convention."

17. On the deeper moral, military, and political difficulties associated with MAD, see Nathan Leites, *Once More About What We Should Not Do Even in the Worst Case: The Assured Destruction Attack* (Santa Monica, CA: California Arms Control and Foreign Policy Seminar, 1974); and David Goldfischer, "Rethinking the Unthinkable after the Cold War: Toward Long-Term Nuclear Policy Planning," *Security Studies* 7, no. 4 (Summer 1998): 165–94.

18. For a fuller discussion of this approach, which U.S. officials are trying to promote, see the testimony of Under Secretary of State John Holum before the U.S. Senate Governmental Affairs Committee, April 12, 2000, and Sokolski, "Post-Cold War Proliferation Controls." http://www.senate.gov/~gov_affairs/041200_holum.htm

19. That the United States has knowingly subsidized foreign proliferating entities is something U.S. officials have openly admitted. See, for example, the testimony of William Reinch, undersecretary of commerce before the U.S. Senate Governmental Affairs Committee, April, 12, 2000. http://www.senate.gov/~gov_affairs/041200_reinsch.htm

20. See Eliot A. Cohen, "A Revolution in Warfare," *Foreign Affairs* 75, no. 2 (March/April 1996): 37–54; and James R. FitzSimonds, "Intelligence and the Revolution in Military Affairs," in *US Intelligence at the Crossroads: Agenda for Reform*, edited by Roy Godson, Ernest R. May, and Gary Schmitt (Washington, D.C.: Brassey's, 1995), 265–87.

21. See Henry S. Rowen, *Catch-Up: Why Poor Countries Are Becoming Richer, Democratic, Increasingly Peaceable, and Sometimes More Dangerous* (Stanford, CA:

Asia/Pacific Research Center, August 1999). An abridged version of this research is contained in Henry Sokolski, ed., *21st Century Weapons Proliferation: Are We Ready?* (London: Frank Cass Publishers, 2001).

22. Ibid. Also, see Francis Fukuyama, *The End of History and the Last Man* (New York: The Free Press, 1992), 37–51; Max Singer and Aaron Wildavsky, *The Real World Order: Zones of Peace, Zones of Turmoil* (Chatham, NJ: Chatham House Publishers, 1993), 14–35; and Strobe Talbott, "Democracy and the National Interest," *Foreign Affairs* (November/December 1996): 47–63.

23. See Singer and Wildavsky, *The Real World Order*, 77–99; Daniel Pipes, "It's Not the Economy Stupid: What the West Needs to Know About the Rise of Radical Islam," *The Washington Post*, July 2, 1995, C2; and Daniel Pipes "Muslim Exceptionalism: Why the End of History Won't Be Easy," in *21st Century Weapons Proliferation*, edited by Henry Sokolski (London: Frank Cass, 2001); and Henry S. Rowen, "Why a Rich, Democratic and (Perhaps) Peaceful Era Is Ahead," in *21st Century Weapons Proliferation*, 108, 112. For additional discussion of the limits on how far liberal democracy and market economy may be able to pacify the future, see Donald Kagan, *On the Origins of War and the Preservation of Peace* (New York: Anchor Books Doubleday, 1996), pp. 1–15 and 566–73.

24. See Janne Nolan, *Guardians of the Arsenal: The Politics of Nuclear Strategy* (New York: New Republic Book, Basic Books, 1989), 3; Glenn Chafetz, "The End of the Cold War and the Future of Nuclear Nonproliferation: An alternative to the Neo-Realist Perspective," *Security Studies*, vol. 2, (Spring/Summer 1993): 128–46; also see George Perkovich, *India's Nuclear Bomb* (Berkeley: University of California Press, 1999), 459, 464.

25. For a more complete history of such efforts and their relation to fighting proliferation, see Sokolski, *Prevailing in a Well-Armed World*, v–26.

APPENDIX I

The Baruch Plan, Presented to the United Nations Atomic Energy Commission, June 14, 1946

My Fellow Members of the United Nations Atomic Energy Commission, and My Fellow Citizens of the World:

We are here to make a choice between the quick and the dead.

That is our business.

Behind the black portent of the new atomic age lies a hope which, seized upon with faith, can work our salvation. If we fail, then we have damned every man to be the slave of Fear. Let us not deceive ourselves: We must elect World Peace or World Destruction.

Science has torn from nature a secret so vast in its potentialities that our minds cower from the terror it creates. Yet terror is not enough to inhibit the use of the atomic bomb. The terror created by weapons has never stopped man from employing them. For each new weapon a defense has been produced, in time. But now we face a condition in which adequate defense does not exist.

Science, which gave us this dread power, shows that it *can* be made a giant help to humanity, but science does *not* show us how to prevent its baleful use. So we have been appointed to obviate that peril by finding a meeting of the minds and the hearts of our peoples. Only in the will of mankind lies the answer.

It is to express this will and make it effective that we have been assembled. We must provide the mechanism to assure that atomic energy is used for peaceful purposes and preclude its use in war. To that end, we must provide immediate, swift, and sure punishment of those who violate the agreements that are reached by the nations. Penalization is essential if peace is to be more than a feverish interlude between wars. And, too, the United Nations can prescribe individual responsibility and punishment on the principles applied at Nürnberg by the Union of Soviet Socialist Republics, the United Kingdom, France, and the United States—a formula certain to benefit the world's future.

In this crisis, we represent not only our governments but, in a larger way, we represent the peoples of the world. We must remember that the peoples do not belong to the governments but that the governments belong to the peoples. We must answer their demands; we must answer the world's longing for peace and security.

In that desire the United States shares ardently and hopefully. The search of science for the absolute weapon has reached fruition in this country. But she stands ready to proscribe and destroy this instrument—to lift its use from death to life—if the world will join in a pact to that end.

In our success lies the promise of a new life, freed from the heart-stopping fears that now beset the world. The beginning of victory for the great ideals for which millions have bled and died lies in building a workable plan. Now we approach fulfillment of the aspirations of mankind. At the end of the road lies the fairer, better, surer life we crave and mean to have.

Only by a lasting peace are liberties and democracies strengthened and deepened. War is their enemy. And it will not do to believe that any of us can escape war's devastation. Victor, vanquished, and neutrals alike are affected physically, economically, and morally.

Against the degradation of war we can erect a safeguard. That is the guerdon for which we reach. Within the scope of the formula we outline here there will be found, to those who seek it, the essential elements of our purpose. Others will see only emptiness. Each of us carries his own mirror in which is reflected hope— or determined desperation—courage or cowardice.

There is a famine throughout the world today. It starves men's bodies. But there is a greater famine—the hunger of men's spirit. That starvation can be cured by the conquest of fear, and the substitution of hope, from which springs faith— faith in each other, faith that we want to work together toward salvation, and determination that those who threaten the peace and safety shall be punished.

The peoples of these democracies gathered here have a particular concern with our answer, for their peoples hate war. They will have a heavy exaction to make of those who fail to provide and escape. They are not afraid of an internationalism that protects; they are unwilling to be fobbed off by mouthings about narrow sovereignty, which is today's phrase for yesterday's isolation.

The basis of a sound foreign policy, in this new age, for all the nations here gathered, is that anything that happens, no matter where or how, which menaces the peace of the world, or the economic stability, concerns each and all of us.

That, roughly, may be said to be the central theme of the United Nations. It is with that thought we begin consideration of the most important subject that can engage mankind—life itself.

Let there be no quibbling about the duty and the responsibility of this group and of the governments we represent. I was moved, in the afternoon of my life, to add my effort to gain the world's quest, by the broad mandate under which we were created. The resolution of the General Assembly, passed January 24, 1946 in London, reads:

"*Section V. Terms of Reference of the Commission*

"The Commission shall proceed with the utmost despatch and enquire into all phases of the problem, and make such recommendations from time to time with respect to them as it finds possible. In particular the Commission shall make specific proposals:

"(a) For extending between all nations the exchange of basic scientific information for peaceful ends;

"(b) For control of atomic energy to the extent necessary to ensure its use only for peaceful purposes;

"(c) For the elimination from national armaments of atomic weapons and of all other major weapons adaptable to mass destruction;

"(d) For effective safeguards by way of inspection and other means to protect complying States against the hazards of violations and evasions.

"The work of the Commission should proceed by separate stages, the successful completion of each of which will develop the necessary confidence of the world before the next stage is undertaken . . ."[1]

Our mandate rests, in text and in spirit, upon the outcome of the Conference in Moscow of Messrs. Molotov of the Union of Soviet Socialist Republics, Bevin of the United Kingdom, and Byrnes of the United States of America. The three Foreign Ministers on December 27, 1945, proposed the establishment of this body.[2]

Their action was animated by a preceding conference in Washington on November 15, 1945, when the President of the United States, associated with Mr. Attlee, Prime Minister of the United Kingdom, and Mr. Mackenzie King, Prime Minister of Canada, stated that international control of the whole field of atomic energy was immediately essential. They proposed the formation of this body. In examining that source, the Agreed Declaration, it will be found that the fathers of the concept recognized the final means of world salvation—the abolition of war. Solemnly they wrote:

"We are aware that the only complete protection for the civilized world from the destructive use of scientific knowledge lies in the prevention of war. No system of safeguards that can be devised will of itself provide an effective guarantee against production of atomic weapons by a nation bent on aggression. Nor can we ignore the possibility of the development of other weapons, or of new methods of warfare, which may constitute as great a threat to civilization as the military use of atomic energy."[3]

Through the historical approach I have outlined, we find ourselves here to test if man can produce, through his will and faith, the miracle of peace, just as he has, through science and skill, the miracle of the atom.

The United States proposes the creation of an International Atomic Development Authority, to which should be entrusted all phases of the development and use of atomic energy, starting with the raw material and including—

1. Managerial control or ownership of all atomic-energy activities potentially dangerous to world security.

2. Power to control, inspect, and license all other atomic activities.

3. The duty of fostering the beneficial uses of atomic energy.

4. Research and development responsibilities of an affirmative character intended to put the Authority in the forefront of atomic knowledge and thus to enable it to comprehend, and therefore to detect, misuse of atomic energy. To be effective, the Authority must itself be the world's leader in the field of atomic

knowledge and development and thus supplement its legal authority with the great power inherent in possession of leadership in knowledge.

I offer this as a basis for beginning our discussion.

But I think the peoples we serve would not believe—and without faith nothing counts—that a treaty, merely outlawing possession or use of the atomic bomb, constitutes effective fulfilment of the instructions to this Commission. Previous failures have been recorded in trying the method of simple renunciation, unsupported by effective guarantees of security and armament limitation. No one would have faith in that approach alone.

Now, if ever, is the time to act for the common good. Public opinion supports a world movement toward security. If I read the signs aright, the peoples want a program not composed merely of pious thoughts but of enforceable sanctions— an international law with teeth in it.

We of this nation, desirous of helping to bring peace to the world and realizing the heavy obligations upon us arising from our possession of the means of producing the bomb and from the fact that it is part of our armament, are prepared to make our full contribution toward effective control of atomic energy.

When an adequate system for control of atomic energy, including the renunciation of the bomb as a weapon, has been agreed upon and put into effective operation and condign punishments set up for violations of the rules of control which are to be stigmatized as international crimes, we propose that—

1. Manufacture of atomic bombs shall stop;

2. Existing bombs shall be disposed of pursuant to the terms of the treaty; and

3. The Authority shall be in possession of full information as to the know-how for the production of atomic energy.

Let me repeat, so as to avoid misunderstanding: My country is ready to make its full contribution toward the end we seek, subject of course to our constitutional processes and to an adequate system of control becoming fully effective, as we finally work it out.

Now as to violations: In the agreement, penalties of as serious a nature as the nations may wish and as immediate and certain in their execution as possible should be fixed for—

1. Illegal possession or use of an atomic bomb;

2. Illegal possession, or separation, of atomic material suitable for use in an atomic bomb;

3. Seizure of any plant or other property belonging to or licensed by the Authority;

4. Willful interference with the activities of the Authority;

5. Creation or operation of dangerous projects in a manner contrary to, or in the absence of, a license granted by the international control body.

It would be a deception, to which I am unwilling to lend myself, were I not to say to you and to our peoples that the matter of punishment lies at the very heart of our present security system. It might as well be admitted, here and now, that the subject goes straight to the veto power contained in the Charter of the United Nations so far as it related to the field of atomic energy. The Charter permits penalization only by concurrence of each of the five great powers—the Union of Soviet Socialist Republics, the United Kingdom, China, France, and the United States.

I want to make very plain that I am concerned here with the veto power only as it affects this particular problem. There must be no veto to protect those who violate their solemn agreements not to develop or use atomic energy for destructive purposes.

The bomb does not wait upon debate. To delay may be to die. The time between violation and preventive action or punishment would be all too short for extended discussion as to the course to be followed.

As matters now stand several years may be necessary for another country to produce a bomb, *de novo*. However, once the basic information is generally known, and the Authority has established producing plants for peaceful purposes in the several countries, an illegal seizure of such a plant might permit a malevolent nation to produce a bomb in 12 months, and if preceded by secret preparation and necessary facilities perhaps even in a much shorter time. The time required—the advance warning given of the possible use of a bomb—can only be generally estimated but obviously will depend upon many factors, including the success with which the Authority has been able to introduce elements of safety in the design of its plants and the degree to which illegal and secret preparation for the military use of atomic energy will have been eliminated. Presumably no nation would think of starting a war with only one bomb.

This shows how imperative speed is in detecting and penalizing violations.

The process of prevention and penalization—a problem of profound statecraft—is, as I read it, implicit in the Moscow statement, signed by the Union of Soviet Socialist Republics, the United States, and the United Kingdom a few months ago.

But before a country is ready to relinquish any winning weapons it must have more than words to reassure it. It must have a guarantee of safety, not only against the offenders in the atomic area but against the illegal users of other weapons—bacteriological, biological, gas—perhaps—why not?—against war itself.

In the elimination of war lies our solution, for only then will nations cease to compete with one another in the production and use of dread "secret" weapons which are evaluated solely by their capacity to kill. This devilish program takes us back not merely to the Dark Ages but from cosmos to chaos. If we succeed in finding a suitable way to control atomic weapons, it is reasonable to hope that we may also preclude the use of other weapons adaptable to mass destruction. When a man learns to say "A" he can, if he chooses, learn the rest of the alphabet too.

Let this be anchored in our minds:

Peace is never long preserved by weight of metal or by an armament race. Peace can be made tranquil and secure only by understanding and agreement fortified by sanctions. We must embrace international cooperation or international disintegration.

Science has taught us how to put the atom to work. But to make it work for good instead of for evil lies in the domain dealing with the principles of human duty. We are now facing a problem more of ethics than of physics.

The solution will require apparent sacrifice in pride and in position, but better pain as the price of peace than death as the price of war.

I now submit the following measures as representing the fundamental features of a plan which would give effect to certain of the conclusions which I have epitomized.

1. General. The Authority should set up a thorough plan for control of the field of atomic energy, through various forms of ownership, dominion, licenses, operation, inspection, research, and management by competent personnel. After this is provided for, there should be as little interference as may be with the economic plans and the present private, corporate, and state relationships in the several countries involved.

2. Raw Materials. The Authority should have as one of its earliest purposes to obtain and maintain complete and accurate information on world supplies of uranium and thorium and to bring them under its dominion. The precise pattern of control for various types of deposits of such materials will have to depend upon the geological, mining, refining, and economic facts involved in different situations.

The Authority should conduct continuous surveys so that it will have the most complete knowledge of the world geology of uranium and thorium. Only after all current information on world sources of uranium and thorium is known to us all can equitable plans be made for their production, refining, and distribution.

3. Primary Production Plants. The Authority should exercise complete managerial control of the production of fissionable materials. This means that it should control and operate all plants producing fissionable materials in dangerous quantities and must own and control the product of these plants.

4. Atomic Explosives. The Authority should be given sole and exclusive right to conduct research in the field of atomic explosives. Research activities in the field of atomic explosives are essential in order that the Authority may keep in the forefront of knowledge in the field of atomic energy and fulfill the objective of preventing illicit manufacture of bombs. Only by maintaining its position as the best-informed agency will the Authority be able to determine the line between intrinsically dangerous and non-dangerous activities.

5. Strategic Distribution of Activities and Materials. The activities entrusted exclusively to the Authority because they are intrinsically dangerous to security should be distributed throughout the world. Similarly, stockpiles of raw materials and fissionable materials should not be centralized.

6. Non-Dangerous Activities. A function of the Authority should be promotion of the peacetime benefits of atomic energy.

Atomic research (except in explosives), the use of research reactors, the production of radioactive tracers by means of non-dangerous reactors, the use of such tracers, and to some extent the production of power should be open to nations and their citizens under reasonable licensing arrangements from the Authority. Denatured materials, whose use we know also requires suitable safeguards, should be furnished for such purposes by the Authority under lease or other arrangement. Denaturing seems to have been overestimated by the public as a safety measure.

7. Definition of Dangerous and Non-Dangerous Activities. Although a reasonable dividing line can be drawn between dangerous and non-dangerous activities, it is not hard and fast. Provision should, therefore, be made to assure constant reexamination of the questions and to permit revision of the dividing line as changing conditions and new discoveries may require.

8. Operations of Dangerous Activities. Any plant dealing with uranium or thorium after it once reaches the potential of dangerous use must be not only subject to the most rigorous and competent inspection by the Authority, but its actual operation shall be under the management, supervision, and control of the Authority.

9. Inspection. By assigning intrinsically dangerous activities exclusively to the Authority, the difficulties of inspection are reduced. If the Authority is the only agency which may lawfully conduct dangerous activities, then visible operation by others than the Authority will constitute an unambiguous danger signal. Inspection will also occur in connection with the licensing functions of the Authority.

10. Freedom of Access. Adequate ingress and egress for all qualified representatives of the Authority must be assured. Many of the inspection activities of the Authority should grow out of, and be incidental to, its other functions. Important measures of inspection will be associated with the tight control of raw materials, for this is a keystone of the plan. The continuing activities of prospecting, survey, and research in relation to raw materials will be designed not only to serve the affirmative development functions of the Authority but also to assure that no surreptitious operations are conducted in the raw-materials field by nations or their citizens.

11. Personnel. The personnel of the Authority should be recruited on a basis of proven competence but also so far as possible on an international basis.

12. Progress by Stages. A primary step in the creation of the system of control is the setting forth, in comprehensive terms, of the functions, responsibilities, powers, and limitations of the Authority. Once a charter for the Authority has been adopted, the Authority and the system of control for which it will be responsible will require time to become fully organized and effective. The plan of control will, therefore, have to come into effect in successive stages. These should be specifically fixed in the charter or means should be otherwise set forth in the charter for transitions from one stage to another, as contemplated in the resolution of the United Nations Assembly which created this Commission.

13. Disclosures. In the deliberations of the United Nations Commission on Atomic Energy, the United States is prepared to make available the information essential to a reasonable understanding of the proposals which it advocates. Further disclosures must be dependent, in the interests of all, upon the effective ratification of the treaty. When the Authority is actually created, the United States will join the other nations in making available the further information essential to that organization for the performance of its functions. As the successive stages of international control are reached, the United States will be prepared to yield, to the extent required by each stage, national control of activities in this field to the Authority.

14. International Control. There will be questions about the extent of control to be allowed to national bodies, when the Authority is established. Purely national authorities for control and development of atomic energy should to the extent necessary for the effective operation of the Authority be subordinate to it. This is neither an endorsement nor a disapproval of the creation of national authorities. The Commission should evolve a clear demarcation of the scope of duties and responsibilities of such national authorities.

And now I end. I have submitted an outline for present discussion. Our consideration will be broadened by the criticism of the United States proposals and by the plans of the other nations, which, it is to be hoped, will be submitted at their early convenience. I and my associates of the United States Delegation will make available to each member of this body books and pamphlets, including the Acheson-Lilienthal report, recently made by the United States Department of State, and the McMahon Committee Monograph No. 1 entitled "Essential Information on Atomic Energy" relating to the McMahon bill recently passed by the United States Senate, which may prove of value in assessing the situation.[4]

All of us are consecrated to making an end of gloom and hopelessness. It will not be an easy job. The way is long and thorny, but supremely worth traveling. All of us want to stand erect, with our faces to the sun, instead of being forced to burrow into the earth, like rats.

The pattern of salvation must be worked out by all for all.

The light at the end of the tunnel is dim, but our path seems to grow brighter as we actually begin our journey. We cannot yet light the way to the end. However, we hope the suggestions of my Government will be illuminating.

Let us keep in mind the exhortation of Abraham Lincoln, whose words, uttered at a moment of shattering national peril, form a complete text for our deliberation. I quote, paraphrasing slightly:

"We cannot escape history. We of this meeting will be remembered in spite of ourselves. No personal significance or insignificance can spare one or another of us. The fiery trial through which we are passing will light us down in honor or dishonor to the latest generation.

"We say we are for Peace. The world will not forget that we say this. We know how to save Peace. The world knows that we do. We, even we here, hold the power and have the responsibility.

"We shall nobly save, or meanly lose, the last, best hope of earth. The way is plain, peaceful, generous, just—a way which, if followed, the world will forever applaud."

My thanks for your attention.

NOTES

1. *Department of State Bulletin*, Feb. 10, 1946, p. 198.
2. Ibid., Dec. 30, 1945, p. 1031.
3. Ibid., Nov. 18, 1945, p. 781.
4. Department of State publication 2498; for excerpts from the Acheson-Lilienthal Report, see *Department of State Bulletin*, Apr. 7, 1946, 553. The text of the McMahon bill is in S. Rept. 1211, 79th Cong.

APPENDIX II

President Eisenhower's Address Before the General Assembly of the United Nations on the Peaceful Uses of Nuclear Energy, December 8, 1953

Madame President, Members of the General Assembly:

When Secretary General Hammarskjöld's invitation to address this General Assembly reached me in Bermuda, I was just beginning a series of conferences with the Prime Ministers and Foreign Ministers of Great Britain and of France. Our subject was some of the problems that beset our world.

During the remainder of the Bermuda Conference, I had constantly in mind that ahead of me lay a great honor. That honor is mine today as I stand here, privileged to address the General Assembly of the United Nations.

At the same time that I appreciate the distinction of addressing you, I have a sense of exhilaration as I look upon this Assembly.

Never before in history has so much hope for so many people been gathered together in a single organization. Your deliberations and decisions during these somber years have already realized part of those hopes.

But the great tests and the great accomplishments still lie ahead. And in the confident expectation of those accomplishments, I would use the office which, for the time being, I hold, to assure you that the Government of the United States will remain steadfast in its support of this body. This we shall do in the conviction that you will provide a great share of the wisdom, the courage, and the faith which can bring to this world lasting peace for all nations, and happiness and well-being for all men.

Clearly, it would not be fitting for me to take this occasion to present to you a unilateral American report on Bermuda. Nevertheless, I assure you that in our deliberations on that lovely island we sought to invoke those same great concepts of universal peace and human dignity which are so clearly etched in your Charter.

Neither would it be a measure of this great opportunity merely to recite, however hopefully, pious platitudes.

I therefore decided that this occasion warranted my saying to you some of the things that have been on the minds and hearts of my legislative and executive associates and on mine for a great many months—thoughts I had originally planned to say primarily to the American people.

I know that the American people share my deep belief that if a danger exists in the world, it is a danger shared by all—and equally, that if hope exists in the mind of one nation, that hope should be shared by all.

Finally, if there is to be advanced any proposal designed to ease even by the smallest measure the tensions of today's world, what more appropriate audience could there be than the members of the United Nations?

I feel impelled to speak today in a language that in a sense is new—one which I, who have spent so much of my life in the military profession, would have preferred never to use.

That new language is the language of atomic warfare.

The atomic age has moved forward at such a pace that every citizen of the world should have some comprehension, at least in comparative terms, of the extent of this development of the utmost significance to every one of us. Clearly, if the peoples of the world are to conduct an intelligent search for peace, they must be armed with the significant facts of today's existence.

My recital of atomic danger and power is necessarily stated in United States terms, for these are the only incontrovertible facts that I know. I need hardly point out to this Assembly, however, that this subject is global, not merely national in character.

On July 16, 1945, the United States set off the world's first atomic explosion. Since that date in 1945, the United States of America has conducted 42 test explosions.

Atomic bombs today are more than 25 times as powerful as the weapons with which the atomic age dawned, while hydrogen weapons are in the ranges of millions of tons of TNT equivalent.

Today, the United States' stockpile of atomic weapons, which, of course, increases daily, exceeds by many times the explosive equivalent of the total of all bombs and all shells that came from every plane and every gun in every theatre of war in all of the years of World War II.

A single air group, whether afloat or land-based, can now deliver to any reachable target a destructive cargo exceeding in power all the bombs that fell on Britain in all of World War II.

In size and variety, the development of atomic weapons has been no less remarkable. The development has been such that atomic weapons have virtually achieved conventional status within our armed services. In the United States, the Army, the Navy, the Air Force and the Marine Corps are all capable of putting this weapon to military use.

But the dread secret, and the fearful engines of atomic might, are not ours alone.

In the first place, the secret is possessed by our friends and allies, Great Britain and Canada, whose scientific genius made a tremendous contribution to our original discoveries, and the designs of atomic bombs.

The secret is also known by the Soviet Union.

The Soviet Union has informed us that, over recent years, it has devoted extensive resources to atomic weapons. During this period, the Soviet Union has exploded a series of atomic devices, including at least one involving thermonuclear reactions.

If at one time the United States possessed what might have been called a monopoly of atomic power, that monopoly ceased to exist several years ago. Therefore, although our earlier start has permitted us to accumulate what is today a great quantitative advantage, the atomic realities of today comprehend two facts of even greater significance.

First, the knowledge now possessed by several nations will eventually be shared by others—possibly all others.

Second, even a vast superiority in numbers of weapons, and a consequent capability of devastating retaliation, is no preventive, of itself, against the fearful material damage and toll of human lives that would be inflicted by surprise aggression.

The free world, at least dimly aware of these facts, has naturally embarked on a large program of warning and defense systems. That program will be accelerated and expanded.

But let no one think that the expenditure of vast sums for weapons and systems of defense can guarantee absolute safety for the cities and citizens of any nation. The awful arithmetic of the atomic bomb does not permit any such easy solution. Even against the most powerful defense, an aggressor in possession of the effective minimum number of atomic bombs for a surprise attack could probably place a sufficient number of his bombs on the chosen targets to cause hideous damage.

Should such an atomic attack be launched against the United States, our reactions would be swift and resolute. But for me to say that the defense capabilities of the United States are such that they could inflict terrible losses upon an aggressor—for me to say that the retaliation capabilities of the United States are so great that such an aggressor's land would be laid waste—all this, while fact, is not the true expression of the purpose and the hope of the United States.

To pause there would be to confirm the hopeless finality of a belief that two atomic colossi are doomed malevolently to eye each other indefinitely across a trembling world. To stop there would be to accept helplessly the probability of civilization destroyed—the annihilation of the irreplaceable heritage of mankind handed down to us generation from generation—and the condemnation of mankind to begin all over again the age-old struggle upward from savagery toward decency, and right, and justice.

Surely no sane member of the human race could discover victory in such desolation. Could anyone wish his name to be coupled by history with such human degradation and destruction.

Occasional pages of history do record the faces of the "Great Destroyers" but the whole book of history reveals mankind's never-ending quest for peace, and mankind's God-given capacity to build.

It is with the book of history, and not with isolated pages, that the United States will ever wish to be identified. My country wants to be constructive, not destructive. It wants agreements, not wars, among nations. It wants itself to live in freedom, and in the confidence that the people of every other nation enjoy equally the right of choosing their own way of life.

So my country's purpose is to help us move out of the dark chamber of horrors into the light, to find a way by which the minds of men, the hopes of men, the souls of men everywhere, can move forward toward peace and happiness and well being.

In this quest, I know that we must not lack patience.

I know that in a world divided, such as ours today, salvation cannot be attained by one dramatic act.

I know that many steps will have to be taken over many months before the world can look at itself one day and truly realize that a new climate of mutually peaceful confidence is abroad in the world.

But I know, above all else, that we must start to take these steps—*now*.

The United States and its allies, Great Britain and France, have over the past months tried to take some of these steps. Let no one say that we shun the conference table.

On the record has long stood the request of the United States, Great Britain, and France to negotiate with the Soviet Union the problems of a divided Germany.

On that record has long stood the request of the same three nations to negotiate an Austrian Peace Treaty.

On the same record still stands the request of the United Nations to negotiate the problems of Korea.

Most recently, we have received from the Soviet Union what is in effect an expression of willingness to hold a Four Power Meeting. Along with our allies, Great Britain and France, we were pleased to see that this note did not contain the unacceptable preconditions previously put forward.

As you already know from our joint Bermuda communique, the United States, Great Britain, and France have agreed promptly to meet with the Soviet Union.

The Government of the United States approaches this conference with hopeful sincerity. We will bend every effort of our minds to the single purpose of emerging from that conference with tangible results toward peace—the only true way of lessening international tension.

We never have, we never will, propose or suggest that the Soviet Union surrender what is rightfully theirs.

We will never say that the peoples of Russia are an enemy with whom we have no desire ever to deal or mingle in friendly and fruitful relationship.

On the contrary, we hope that this coming Conference may initiate a relationship with the Soviet Union which will eventually bring about a free intermingling of the peoples of the East and of the West—the one sure, human way of developing the understanding required for confident and peaceful relations.

Instead of the discontent which is now settling upon Eastern Germany, occupied Austria, and the countries of Eastern Europe, we seek a harmonious family of free European nations, with none a threat to the other, and least of all a threat to the peoples of Russia.

Beyond the turmoil and strife and misery of Asia, we seek peaceful opportunity for these peoples to develop their natural resources and to elevate their lives.

These are not idle words or shallow visions. Behind them lies a story of nations lately come to independence, not as a result of war, but through free grant or peaceful negotiation. There is a record, already written, of assistance gladly given by nations of the West to needy peoples, and to those suffering the temporary effects of famine, drought, and natural disaster.

These are deeds of peace. They speak more loudly than promises or protestations of peaceful intent.

But I do not wish to rest either upon the reiteration of past proposals or the restatement of past deeds. The gravity of the time is such that every new avenue of peace, no matter how dimly discernible, should be explored.

There is at least one new avenue of peace which has not yet been well explored—an avenue now laid out by the General Assembly of the United Nations.

In its resolution of November 18th, 1953, this General Assembly suggested—and I quote—"that the Disarmament Commission study the desirability of establishing a sub-committee consisting of representatives of the Powers principally involved, which should seek in private an acceptable solution . . . and report on such a solution to the General Assembly and to the Security Council not later than 1 September 1954."

The United States, heeding the suggestion of the General Assembly of the United Nations, is instantly prepared to meet privately with such other countries as may be "principally involved," to seek "an acceptable solution" to the atomic armaments race which overshadows not only the peace, but the very life, of the world.

We shall carry into these private or diplomatic talks a new conception.

The United States would seek more than the mere reduction or elimination of atomic materials for military purposes.

It is not enough to take this weapon out of the hands of the soldiers. It must be put into the hands of those who will know how to strip its military casing and adapt it to the arts of peace.

The United States knows that if the fearful trend of atomic military build up can be reversed, this greatest of destructive forces can be developed into a great boon, for the benefit of all mankind.

The United States knows that peaceful power from atomic energy is no dream of the future. That capability, already proved, is here—now—today. Who can doubt, if the entire body of the world's scientists and engineers had adequate amounts of fissionable material with which to test and develop their ideas, that this capability would rapidly be transformed into universal, efficient, and economic usage.

To hasten the day when fear of the atom will begin to disappear from the minds of people, and the governments of the East and West, there are certain steps that can be taken now.

I therefore make the following proposals:

The Governments principally involved, to the extent permitted by elementary prudence, to begin now and continue to make joint contributions from their stockpiles of normal uranium and fissionable materials to an International Atomic Energy Agency. We would expect that such an agency would be set up under the aegis of the United Nations.

The ratios of contributions, the procedures and other details would properly be within the scope of the "private conversations" I have referred to earlier.

The United States is prepared to undertake these explorations in good faith. Any partner of the United States acting in the same good faith will find the United States a not unreasonable or ungenerous associate.

Undoubtedly initial and early contributions to this plan would be small in quantity. However, the proposal has the great virtue that it can be undertaken without the irritations and mutual suspicions incident to any attempt to set up a completely acceptable system of worldwide inspection and control.

The Atomic Energy Agency could be made responsible for the impounding, storage, and protection of the contributed fissionable and other materials. The ingenuity of our scientists will provide special safe conditions under which such a bank of fissionable material can be made essentially immune to surprise seizure.

The more important responsibility of this Atomic Energy Agency would be to devise methods whereby this fissionable material would be allocated to serve the peaceful pursuits of mankind. Experts would be mobilized to apply atomic energy to the needs of agriculture, medicine, and other peaceful activities. A special purpose would be to provide abundant electrical energy in the power-starved areas of the world. Thus the contributing powers would be dedicating some of their strength to serve the needs rather than the fears of mankind.

The United States would be more than willing—it would be proud to take up with others "principally involved" the development of plans whereby such peaceful use of atomic energy would be expedited.

Of those "principally involved" the Soviet Union must, of course, be one.

I would be prepared to submit to the Congress of the United States, and with every expectation of approval, any such plan that would:

First—encourage worldwide investigation into the most effective peacetime uses of fissionable material, and with the certainty that they had all the material needed for the conduct of all experiments that were appropriate;

Second—begin to diminish the potential destructive power of the world's atomic stockpiles;

Third—allow all peoples of all nations to see that, in this enlightened age, the great powers of the earth, both of the East and of the West, are interested in human aspirations first, rather than in building up the armaments of war;

Fourth—open up a new channel for peaceful discussion, and initiate at least a new approach to the many difficult problems that must be solved in both private and public conversations, if the world is to shake off the inertia imposed by fear, and is to make positive progress toward peace.

Against the dark background of the atomic bomb, the United States does not wish merely to present strength, but also the desire and the hope for peace.

The coming months will be fraught with fateful decisions. In this Assembly; in the capitals and military headquarters of the world; in the hearts of men everywhere, be they governors or governed, may they be the decisions which will lead this world out of fear and into peace.

To the making of these fateful decisions, the United States pledges before you—and therefore before the world—its determination to help solve the fearful atomic dilemma—and to devote its entire heart and mind to find the way by which the miraculous inventiveness of man shall not be dedicated to his death, but consecrated to his life.

I again thank the delegates for the great honor they have done me, in inviting me to appear before them, and in listening to me so courteously. Thank you.

Note: The president's opening words referred to Mme. Vijaya Pandit, president of the United Nations General Assembly.

APPENDIX III

Treaty on the Non-Proliferation of Nuclear Weapons

Signed at Washington, London, and Moscow July 1, 1968
Ratification advised by U.S. Senate March 13, 1969
Ratified by U.S. President November 24, 1969
U.S. ratification deposited at Washington, London, and Moscow March 5, 1970
Proclaimed by U.S. President March 5, 1970
Entered into force March 5, 1970

The States concluding this Treaty, hereinafter referred to as the "Parties to the Treaty,"

Considering the devastation that would be visited upon all mankind by a nuclear war and the consequent need to make every effort to avert the danger of such a war and to take measures to safeguard the security of peoples,

Believing that the proliferation of nuclear weapons would seriously enhance the danger of nuclear war,

In conformity with resolutions of the United Nations General Assembly calling for the conclusion of an agreement on the prevention of wider dissemination of nuclear weapons, Undertaking to cooperate in facilitating the application of International Atomic Energy Agency safeguards on peaceful nuclear activities,

Expressing their support for research, development and other efforts to further the application, within the framework of the International Atomic Energy Agency safeguards system, of the principle of safeguarding effectively the flow of source and special fissionable materials by use of instruments and other techniques at certain strategic points,

Affirming the principle that the benefits of peaceful applications of nuclear technology, including any technological by-products which may be derived by nuclear-weapon States from the development of nuclear explosive devices, should be available for peaceful purposes to all Parties of the Treaty, whether nuclear-weapon or non-nuclear weapon States,

Convinced that, in furtherance of this principle, all Parties to the Treaty are entitled to participate in the fullest possible exchange of scientific information for, and to contribute alone or in cooperation with other States to, the further development of the applications of atomic energy for peaceful purposes,

Declaring their intention to achieve at the earliest possible date the cessation of the nuclear arms race and to undertake effective measures in the direction of nuclear disarmament,

Urging the cooperation of all States in the attainment of this objective,

Recalling the determination expressed by the Parties to the 1963 Treaty banning nuclear weapon tests in the atmosphere, in outer space and under water in its Preamble to seek to achieve the discontinuance of all test explosions of nuclear weapons for all time and to continue negotiations to this end,

Desiring to further the easing of international tension and the strengthening of trust between States in order to facilitate the cessation of the manufacture of nuclear weapons, the liquidation of all their existing stockpiles, and the elimination from national arsenals of nuclear weapons and the means of their delivery pursuant to a Treaty on general and complete disarmament under strict and effective international control,

Recalling that, in accordance with the Charter of the United Nations, States must refrain in their international relations from the threat or use of force against the territorial integrity or political independence of any State, or in any other manner inconsistent with the Purposes of the United Nations, and that the establishment and maintenance of international peace and security are to be promoted with the least diversion for armaments of the worlds human and economic resources,

Have agreed as follows:

ARTICLE I

Each nuclear-weapon State Party to the Treaty undertakes not to transfer to any recipient whatsoever nuclear weapons or other nuclear explosive devices or control over such weapons or explosive devices directly, or indirectly; and not in any way to assist, encourage, or induce any non-nuclear weapon State to manufacture or otherwise acquire nuclear weapons or other nuclear explosive devices, or control over such weapons or explosive devices.

ARTICLE II

Each non-nuclear-weapon State Party to the Treaty undertakes not to receive the transfer from any transferor whatsoever of nuclear weapons or other nuclear explosive devices or of control over such weapons or explosive devices directly, or indirectly; not to manufacture or otherwise acquire nuclear weapons or other nuclear explosive devices; and not to seek or receive any assistance in the manufacture of nuclear weapons or other nuclear explosive devices.

ARTICLE III

1. Each non-nuclear-weapon State Party to the Treaty undertakes to accept safeguards, as set forth in an agreement to be negotiated and concluded with the International Atomic Energy Agency in accordance with the Statute of the International Atomic Energy Agency and the Agency's safeguards system, for the exclusive purpose of verification of the fulfillment of its obligations assumed

under this Treaty with a view to preventing diversion of nuclear energy from peaceful uses to nuclear weapons or other nuclear explosive devices. Procedures for the safeguards required by this article shall be followed with respect to source or special fissionable material whether it is being produced, processed or used in any principal nuclear facility or is outside any such facility. The safeguards required by this article shall be applied to all source or special fissionable material in all peaceful nuclear activities within the territory of such State, under its jurisdiction, or carried out under its control anywhere.

2. Each State Party to the Treaty undertakes not to provide: (a) source or special fissionable material, or (b) equipment or material especially designed or prepared for the processing, use or production of special fissionable material, to any non-nuclear-weapon State for peaceful purposes, unless the source or special fissionable material shall be subject to the safeguards required by this article.

3. The safeguards required by this article shall be implemented in a manner designed to comply with article IV of this Treaty, and to avoid hampering the economic or technological development of the Parties or international cooperation in the field of peaceful nuclear activities, including the international exchange of nuclear material and equipment for the processing, use or production of nuclear material for peaceful purposes in accordance with the provisions of this article and the principle of safeguarding set forth in the Preamble of the Treaty.

4. Non-nuclear-weapon States Party to the Treaty shall conclude agreements with the International Atomic Energy Agency to meet the requirements of this article either individually or together with other States in accordance with the Statute of the International Atomic Energy Agency. Negotiation of such agreements shall commence within 180 days from the original entry into force of this Treaty. For States depositing their instruments of ratification or accession after the 180-day period, negotiation of such agreements shall commence not later than the date of such deposit. Such agreements shall enter into force not later than eighteen months after the date of initiation of negotiations.

ARTICLE IV

1. Nothing in this Treaty shall be interpreted as affecting the inalienable right of all the Parties to the Treaty to develop research, production and use of nuclear energy for peaceful purposes without discrimination and in conformity with articles I and II of this Treaty.

2. All the Parties to the Treaty undertake to facilitate, and have the right to participate in, the fullest possible exchange of equipment, materials and scientific and technological information for the peaceful uses of nuclear energy. Parties to the Treaty in a position to do so shall also cooperate in contributing alone or together with other States or international organizations to the further development of the applications of nuclear energy for peaceful purposes, especially in the territories of non-nuclear-weapon States Party to the Treaty, with due consideration for the needs of the developing areas of the world.

ARTICLE V

Each party to the Treaty undertakes to take appropriate measures to ensure that, in accordance with this Treaty, under appropriate international observation and through appropriate international procedures, potential benefits from any peaceful applications of nuclear explosions will be made available to non-nuclear-weapon States Party to the Treaty on a nondiscriminatory basis and that the charge to such Parties for the explosive devices used will be as low as possible and exclude any charge for research and development. Non-nuclear-weapon States Party to the Treaty shall be able to obtain such benefits, pursuant to a special international agreement or agreements, through an appropriate international body with adequate representation of non-nuclear-weapon States. Negotiations on this subject shall commence as soon as possible after the Treaty enters into force. Non-nuclear-weapon States Party to the Treaty so desiring may also obtain such benefits pursuant to bilateral agreements.

ARTICLE VI

Each of the Parties to the Treaty undertakes to pursue negotiations in good faith on effective measures relating to cessation of the nuclear arms race at an early date and to nuclear disarmament, and on a Treaty on general and complete disarmament under strict and effective international control.

ARTICLE VII

Nothing in this Treaty affects the right of any group of States to conclude regional treaties in order to assure the total absence of nuclear weapons in their respective territories.

ARTICLE VIII

1. Any Party to the Treaty may propose amendments to this Treaty. The text of any proposed amendment shall be submitted to the Depositary Governments which shall circulate it to all Parties to the Treaty. Thereupon, if requested to do so by one-third or more of the Parties to the Treaty, the Depositary Governments shall convene a conference, to which they shall invite all the Parties to the Treaty, to consider such an amendment.

2. Any amendment to this Treaty must be approved by a majority of the votes of all the Parties to the Treaty, including the votes of all nuclear-weapon States Party to the Treaty and all other Parties which, on the date the amendment is circulated, are members of the Board of Governors of the International Atomic Energy Agency. The amendment shall enter into force for each Party that deposits its instrument of ratification of the amendment upon the deposit of such instruments of ratification by a majority of all the Parties, including the instruments of ratification of all nuclear-weapon States Party to the Treaty and all other Parties which, on the date the amendment is circulated, are members of the Board of Governors of the International Atomic Energy Agency. Thereafter, it shall enter into force for any other Party upon the deposit of its instrument of ratification of the amendment.

3. Five years after the entry into force of this Treaty, a conference of Parties to the Treaty shall be held in Geneva, Switzerland, in order to review the operation of this Treaty with a view to assuring that the purposes of the Preamble and the provisions of the Treaty are being realized. At intervals of five years thereafter, a majority of the Parties to the Treaty may obtain, by submitting a proposal to this effect to the Depositary Governments, the convening of further conferences with the same objective of reviewing the operation of the Treaty.

ARTICLE IX

1. This Treaty shall be open to all States for signature. Any State which does not sign the Treaty before its entry into force in accordance with paragraph 3 of this article may accede to it at any time.

2. This Treaty shall be subject to ratification by signatory States. Instruments

of ratification and instruments of accession shall be deposited with the Governments of the United States of America, the United Kingdom of Great Britain and Northern Ireland and the Union of Soviet Socialist Republics, which are hereby designated the Depositary Governments.

3. This Treaty shall enter into force after its ratification by the States, the Governments of which are designated Depositaries of the Treaty, and forty other States signatory to this Treaty and the deposit of their instruments of ratification. For the purposes of this Treaty, a nuclear-weapon State is one which has manufactured and exploded a nuclear weapon or other nuclear explosive device prior to January 1, 1967.

4. For States whose instruments of ratification or accession are deposited subsequent to the entry into force of this Treaty, it shall enter into force on the date of the deposit of their instruments of ratification or accession.

5. The Depositary Governments shall promptly inform all signatory and acceding States of the date of each signature, the date of deposit of each instrument of ratification or of accession, the date of the entry into force of this Treaty, and the date of receipt of any requests for convening a conference or other notices.

6. This Treaty shall be registered by the Depositary Governments pursuant to article 102 of the Charter of the United Nations.

ARTICLE X

1. Each Party shall in exercising its national sovereignty have the right to withdraw from the Treaty if it decides that extraordinary events, related to the subject matter of this Treaty, have jeopardized the supreme interests of its country. It shall give notice of such withdrawal to all other Parties to the Treaty and to the United Nations Security Council three months in advance. Such notice shall include a statement of the extraordinary events it regards as having jeopardized its supreme interests.

2. Twenty-five years after the entry into force of the Treaty, a conference shall be convened to decide whether the Treaty shall continue in force indefinitely, or shall be extended for an additional fixed period or periods. This decision shall be taken by a majority of the Parties to the Treaty.

ARTICLE XI

This Treaty, the English, Russian, French, Spanish and Chinese texts of which are equally authentic, shall be deposited in the archives of the Depositary Governments. Duly certified copies of this Treaty shall be transmitted by the Depositary Governments to the Governments of the signatory and acceding States.

IN WITNESS WHEREOF the undersigned, duly authorized, have signed this Treaty.

DONE in triplicate, at the cities of Washington, London and Moscow, this first day of July one thousand nine hundred sixty-eight.

APPENDIX IV

Multilateral Export Control Regimes: Membership and Related Websites[1]

Country	The Zangger Committee	The Nuclear Suppliers Group	The Australia Group	The Missile Technology Control Regime	The Wassenaar Arrangement
Argentina	√	√	√	√	√
Australia	√	√	√	√	√
Austria	√	√	√	√	√
Belgium	√	√	√	√	√
Brazil		√		√	
Bulgaria	√	√			√
Canada	√	√	√	√	√
China	√				
Czech Republic	√	√	√	√	√
Denmark	√	√	√	√	√
Finland	√	√	√	√	√
France	√	√	√	√	√
Germany	√	√	√	√	√
Greece	√	√	√	√	√
Hungary	√	√	√	√	√
Iceland			√	√	

Ireland	√	√	√	√	√
Italy	√	√	√	√	√
Japan	√	√	√	√	√
Latvia		√			
Luxembourg	√	√	√	√	√
Netherlands	√	√	√	√	√
New Zealand		√	√	√	√
Norway	√	√	√	√	√
Poland	√	√	√	√	√
Portugal	√	√	√	√	√
Romania	√	√	√		√
Russia	√	√		√	√
Slovakia	√	√	√		√
South Africa	√	√		√	
South Korea	√	√	√		√
Spain	√	√	√	√	√
Sweden	√	√	√	√	√
Switzerland	√	√	√	√	√
Turkey	√			√	√
Ukraine	√	√		√	√
United Kingdom	√	√	√	√	√
United States	√	√	√	√	√

NOTE

1. For more information on these multilateral export control groups, including pertinent texts, documents and news for each, see:

Zangger Committee: http://sun00781.dn.net/nuke/control/zangger/
                            index.html

Nuclear Suppliers Group: http://sun00781.dn.net/nuke/control/nsg/text/
                            index.html

Australia Group: http://sun00781.dn.net/nuke/control/ag/docs/
                            index.html

Missile Technology Control Regime:	http://sun00781.dn.net/nuke/control/mtcr/
Wassenaar Arrangement:	http://sun00781.nd.net/nuke/control/wassenaar/ index.html http://www.wassenaar.org

Remarks by Honorable Les Aspin, Secretary of Defense, National Academy of Sciences Committee on International Security and Arms Control, December 7, 1993

Thank you very much, Dr. Alberts, and thank all of you for coming this morning. I'm particularly pleased to be able to talk about this important topic before this audience because I know many of you have thought about this. It's something that's going to take all our best efforts.

The national security requirements of the United States have undergone fundamental change in just a few short years. We won the Cold War. The Soviet threat that dominated our strategy, doctrine, weapons acquisition and force structure for so long is gone. With it has gone the threat of global war. But history did not end with that victory, and neither did threats to the United States, its people and its interests.

As part of the Bottom Up Review we began to think seriously about what threats we really faced in this new era. We came up with four chief threats to the United States. First, a new danger posed by the increased threat of proliferation of nuclear weapons and other weapons of mass destruction. Second, regional dangers posed by the threat of aggression by powers such as Saddam Hussein's Iraq. Third, the danger that democratic and market reforms will fail in the former Soviet Union, Eastern Europe and elsewhere. And finally, we recognize an economic danger to our national security. In the short run our security is protected by a strong military, but in the long run it will be protected by a strong economy.

Of these dangers, the one that most urgently and directly threatens America at home and American interests abroad is the new nuclear danger. The old nuclear danger we faced was thousands of warheads in the Soviet Union. The new nuclear danger we face is perhaps a handful of nuclear devices in the hands of rogue states or even terrorist groups. The engine of this new danger is proliferation.

Let us recall briefly how we dealt with the old nuclear danger—the nuclear danger of the Cold War era. We had three approaches—deterrence, arms control and a nonproliferation policy based on prevention. They worked.

Our policy of deterrence was aimed primarily at the Soviet Union. Our aim was to guarantee by the structure and disposition of our own nuclear forces that a nuclear attack on the United States or its allies would bring no profit, and thus deter it.

We sought to stabilize these arsenals through arms control and eventually to shrink them through arms reduction. Our nonproliferation policy was aimed at preventing the spread of nuclear weapons by persuading most nations not to go nuclear, and denying the materials and know-how to make bombs to those who pursued them. And in fact, these weapons did not spread as quickly as many suggested.

But that was then and this is now. And now we face the potential of a greatly increased proliferation problem. This increase is the product of two new developments. The first arises from the break-up of the former Soviet Union. The second concerns the nature of technology diffusion in this new era. Each of these developments profoundly changes the nature of the proliferation problem.

Let's look at the former Soviet Union. The continued existence of the former Soviet Union's arsenal amidst revolutionary change gives rise to four potential proliferation problems.

First, and most obvious, is that nuclear weapons are now deployed on the territory of four states. Before, there was one. The safe and security transport and dismantlement of these weapons is one of the U.S. Government's highest priorities.

Second, we have the potential for what I call "loose nukes." In a time of profound transition in the former Soviet Union, it is possible that nuclear weapons, or the material or technology to make them could find their way to a nuclear black market.

Third, nuclear and other weapons expertise for hire could go to would-be proliferators.

Fourth, whatever restraint the former Soviet Union exercised over its client states with nuclear ambitions, such as North Korea, is much diminished. Regional power balances have been disrupted and old ethnic conflicts have re-emerged.

The other new development that exacerbates today's proliferation problem is a by-product of growth in world trade and the rising tide of technology everywhere.

The world economy today is characterized by an ever increasing volume of trade leading to ever greater diffusion of technology. Simply put, this will make it harder and harder to detect illicit diversions of materials and technology useful for weapons development.

Moreover, many potential aggressors no longer have to import all the sophisticated technology they need. They are "growing" it at home. The growth of indigenous technology can completely change the nonproliferation equation.

Potential proliferators are sometimes said to be "several decades behind the West." This is not much comfort. If a would-be nuclear nation is four decades behind in 1993 then it is at the same technological level as the United States was in 1953. By 1953, the United States had fission weapons. We were building intercontinental range bombers and were developing intercontinental missiles.

Realize, too, that most of the thermonuclear weapons in the United States arsenal today were designed in the 1960s using computers that were then known as "super computers." These same "super computers" are no more powerful than today's laptop personal computers that you can pick up at the store or order through the catalog.

These new developments tell us a couple of very important things. The first, of course, is that we face a bigger proliferation danger than we've ever faced before. But second, and most important, is that a policy of prevention through denial won't be enough to cope with the potential of tomorrow's proliferators.

In concrete terms, here is where we stand today. More than a score of countries—many of them hostile to the United States, our friends and our allies— have now or are developing nuclear, biological and/or chemical weapons—and the means to deliver them. More than 12 countries have operational ballistic missiles and others have programs to develop them.

Weapons of mass destruction may directly threaten our forces in the field, and in a more subtle way threaten the effective use of those forces. In some ways, in fact, the role of nuclear weapons in the U.S. scheme of things has completely changed.

During the Cold War, our principal adversary had conventional forces in Europe that were numerically superior. For us, nuclear weapons were the equalizer. The threat to use them was present and was used to compensate for our smaller numbers of conventional forces. Today, nuclear weapons can still be the equalizer against superior conventional forces. But today it is the United States that has unmatched conventional military power, and it is our potential adversaries who may attain nuclear weapons. We're the ones who could wind up being the equalizee.

And it's not just nuclear weapons. All the potential threat nations are at least capable of producing biological and chemical agents. They might not have usable weapons yet, and they might not use them if they do. But our commanders will have to assume that U.S. forces are threatened.

So the threat is real and it is upon us today. President Clinton directed the world's attention to it in his speech to the United Nations General Assembly in September. He said, "One of our most urgent priorities must be attacking the proliferation of weapons of mass destruction, whether they are nuclear, chemical or biological; and the ballistic missiles that can rain them down on populations hundreds of miles away. . . . If we do not stem the proliferation of the world's deadliest weapons, no democracy can feel secure."

To respond to the President, we have created the Defense Counterproliferation Initiative. With this initiative, we are making the essential change demanded by this increased threat. We are adding the task of protection to the task of prevention.

In past administrations, the emphasis was on prevention. The policy of nonproliferation combined global diplomacy and regional security efforts with the denial of material and know-how to would-be proliferators. Prevention remains our pre-eminent goal. In North Korea, for example, our goals are still a nonnuclear peninsula and a strong nonproliferation regime.

The Defense Counterproliferation Initiative in no way means we will lessen our nonproliferation efforts. In fact, DoD's work will strengthen prevention. What the Defense Counterproliferation Initiative recognizes, however, is that proliferation may still occur. Thus, we are adding protection as a major policy goal.

The chart shows how the two—prevention and protection—combine to make a complete attack on the problem. On the left, we have the policy instruments for prevention. On the right are the steps we take to protect if proliferation occurs. What's new is the emphasis on the right side of the chart where the Defense Department has a special responsibility.

At the heart of the Defense Counterproliferation Initiative, therefore, is a drive to develop new military capabilities to deal with this new threat. It has five elements: One, creation of the new mission by the President; two, changing what we buy to meet the threat; three, planning to fight wars differently; four, changing how we collect intelligence and what intelligence we collect; and finally, five, doing all these things with our allies.

Let's look at each in turn.

First point; new mission. President Clinton not only recognized the danger of the new threat, he gave us this new mission to cope with it. We have issued defense planning guidance to the services to make sure everyone understands what the President wants. I have organized my own staff to reflect the importance of the new mission with the new position of Assistant Secretary of Defense for Nuclear Security and Counterproliferation.

Second point; what we buy. We are reviewing all relevant programs to see what we can do better. For example, we're looking at improved non-nuclear penetrating munitions to deal with underground installations. Saddam Hussein, you'll recall, was building a lot of underground refuges because normal structures were totally vulnerable to our precision air strikes. We cannot let future Saddams escape attack. We're also working hard on better ways to hunt mobile missiles after our difficulties in finding Scuds during the Gulf War. And of course, we have reoriented the Strategic Defense Initiative into the Ballistic Missile Defense Organization so that it concentrates on responding to theater ballistic missile threats that are here today.

We've also proposed a clarification in the ABM treaty. It would allow us to develop and test a theater missile defense system to meet a real threat without undermining an important agreement. This is an essential element of our counterproliferation strategy.

Third point; how we fight wars. We are developing guidance for dealing with this new threat. We have directed the services to tell us how prepared they are for it. The Chairman of the Joint Chiefs of Staff and our regional commanders in chief—our CINCs—are developing a military planning process for dealing with adversaries who have weapons of mass destruction.

And our concerns are by no means limited to the nuclear threat. We have a new Joint Office to oversee all DoD biological defense programs. This is the first time the department has organized its collective expertise to deal with the tough biological defense problems we face.

Fourth point; intelligence. After the war with Iraq, we discovered that Saddam Hussein had a much more extensive nuclear weapons program going than we knew. Moreover, we learned during the war that we had failed to destroy his biological and chemical warfare efforts. We do not want to be caught like that again, so we are working to improve our counterproliferation intelligence.

As a first step, we are pursuing an arrangement with the director of central intelligence to establish a new deputy director for military support in the Intelligence Community's Nonproliferation Center. And we're tripling the number of Defense Department experts assigned to the center. We're looking for intelligence that is useful militarily, not only diplomatically.

Fifth point; international cooperation. Our allies and security partners around the world have as much to be concerned about as we do. We have tabled an initiative with NATO to increase alliance efforts against proliferation of weapons of mass destruction.

We are also cooperating actively with the Japanese on deployment of theater missile defense systems there, and possibly on developing such systems together.

We are paying special attention to the dangerous potential problem of weapons and nuclear material proliferating from the Soviet Union. Under the Nunn-Lugar program, we are helping Russia, Belarus, Ukraine and Kazakhstan with the safe and secure dismantling of their nuclear weapons. And we're helping them improve the security of fissile material in both weapons and civilian nuclear facilities by helping them set up material control and accounting systems.

We are even including Russia in our attempt to reshape export controls on sensitive technology. The control system used to be aimed at the Eastern Bloc. Now we are incorporating former Eastern Bloc countries in our efforts to impede would-be proliferators. The Defense Department can play a constructive role in balancing economics and security here. In this effort, we have been guided by the excellent work conducted by the National Academy of Sciences.

To sum up, we've undertaken a new mission. For many years we planned to counter the weapons of mass destruction of the former Soviet Union. Now, we've recognized a new problem and we're acting to meet it with counterproliferation. At the same time, our initiative complements nonproliferation in three important ways. It promotes consensus on the gravity of the threat, helping to maintain the international nonproliferation effort. It reduces the military utility of weapons of mass destruction, while nonproliferation keeps up the price, making them less attractive to the proliferator. And it reduces the vulnerability of the neighbors of those holding these weapons, further reducing the motive to acquire them in self-defense.

We are in a new era. We have released our Bottom Up Review that provided a blueprint for our conventional forces for the years ahead. Our Defense Counterproliferation Initiative will allow us to deal with the number one threat identified in the BUR, and it will help provide the real strength America needs to meet the dangers we face. The public expects nothing less from its Department of Defense than the right responses to the new world.

Thank you.

Responding to the Proliferation Threat

Prevention					Protection		
Dissuasion	**Denial**	**Arms Control**	**International Pressure**	**Defusing**	**Deterrence**	**Offense**	**Defense**
- Emphasizing economic, political, and military costs of proliferation - Positive/negative security assurance and guarantees - Security assistance - Public Diplomacy	-Export controls - Interdiction -Disruption of supply networks	- NPT, BWC, CWC, - Nuclear free zones - CSBMs - "Rolling back" Argentine missiles, South African nukes,... -Inspections and monitoring	- Sanctions - Isolation - Publicizing violations - Intelligence sharing to persuade others of the danger	- Cooperative dismantlement - Safety and security enhancements - Stabilizing measures - CSBMs	- Small nuclear arsenals - CW - BW - "Undeterrables"	- Underground structures - SCUD hunting - Contamination problems	- TMD - BW vaccines - Strategic and tactical warning - Unconventional delivery, counterterrorism - NEST - Border /perimeter control

Special DoD Responsibility

DoD Shares Interagency Responsibility

Selected Bibliography

PUBLIC PAPERS AND GOVERNMENT PUBLICATIONS

Commission to Assess the Ballistic Missile Threat to the United States, *Report of the Commission to Assess the Ballistic Missile Threat to the United States*, pursuant to Public Law 201, 104th Congress, July 15, 1998.

Commission to Assess the Organization of the Federal Government to Combat the Proliferation of Weapons of Mass Destruction, *Combating Proliferation of Weapons of Mass Destruction*, pursuant to Public Law 293, 104th Congress, July 14, 1999.

IAEA Statute Conference Debates. IAEA/CS/OR.35 and IAEA/CS/OR.37, 1956.

Lilienthal, David. *A Report on the International Control of Atomic Energy*. Washington, D.C.: USGPO, March 16, 1946.

Office of the Secretary of Defense. *Proliferation: Threat and Response*. Washington, D.C.: USGPO, November 1997.

Papers of Dwight D. Eisenhower, Dwight D. Eisenhower Library, Abilene, Kansas.

Papers of C. D. Jackson, Dwight D. Eisenhower Library, Abilene, Kansas.

United Nations Department of Political and Security Council Affairs. *The United Nations and Disarmament 1945–1970*. New York: United Nations Publications, 1971.

U.S. Arms Control and Disarmament Agency. *Documents on Disarmament, 1968*. Washington, D.C.: USGPO, 1969.

———. *Documents on Disarmament, 1967*. Washington, D.C.: USGPO, 1968.

———. *Documents on Disarmament, 1966*. Washington, D.C.: USGPO, 1967.

———. *Documents on Disarmament, 1965*. Washington, D.C.: USGPO, 1966.

———. *Documents on Disarmament, 1964*. Washington, D.C.: USGPO, 1965.

———. *Documents on Disarmament, 1963.* Washington, D.C.: USGPO, 1964.

———. *Documents on Disarmament, 1962.* Washington, D.C.: USGPO, 1963.

———. *Documents on Disarmament, 1961.* Washington, D.C.: USGPO, 1962.

U.S. Atomic Energy Commission. *In the Matter of J. Robert Oppenheimer: Transcript of Hearings Before Personnel Security Board, April 12, 1954, Through May 6, 1954.* Washington, D.C.: USGPO, 1954.

U.S. Congress. Congressional Research Service. *Nuclear Proliferation Factbook.* Washington, D.C.: USGPO, 1995.

U.S. Congress. House, Select Committee on U.S. National Security and Military/ Commercial Concerns with the People's Republic of China. *U.S. National Security and Military/Commercial Concerns with the Peoples Republic of China.* Vols. I–III. Washington, D.C.: USGPO, May 1999.

U.S. Congress. Joint Committee on Atomic Energy. *Review of the International Atomic Policies and Programs of the United States.* Robert McKinney. Joint Committee Print. Washington, D.C.: USGPO, 1960.

U.S. Department of Defense. Office of the Secretary of Defense. *Proliferation: Threat and Response.* Washington, D.C.: USGPO, 1997.

U.S. Department of State. "Armaments and American Policy: A Report of the Panel of Consultants on Disarmament of the Department of State." State Department Archives, file number 330.13/1–1553, January 15, 1953.

———. *Documents on Disarmament 1945–1959.* 2 vols. Washington, D.C.: USGPO, 1960.

———. *The Foreign Relations of the United States, 1952–54.* Vol. 2. Washington, D.C.: USGPO, 1990.

———. *The Foreign Relations of the United States, Diplomatic Papers, 1950.* Washington, D.C.: USGPO, 1977.

BOOKS

Acheson, Dean. *Present at the Creation.* New York: W. W. Norton, 1969.

Adams, Sherman. *Firsthand Report.* New York: Harper and Brothers, 1961.

Albright, David, and Kevin O'Neill, eds. *The Challenges of Fissile Material Control.* Washington, D.C.: Institute for Science and International Security, 1999.

———. *Solving the North Korean Nuclear Puzzle.* Washington, D.C.: Institute for Science and International Security, 2000.

Albright, David, Frans Berkhout, and William Walker. *Plutonium and Highly Enriched Uranium 1996: World Inventories, Capabilities and Policies.* Oxford: Oxford University Press, 1997.

Allardice, Corbin, and Edward Trapnell. *The Atomic Energy Commission.* New York: Praeger Publishers, 1974.

Beaton, Leonard. *Must the Bomb Spread?* Middlesex, UK: Penguin Books, 1966.

Betts, Richard K. *Nuclear Blackmail and Nuclear Balance.* Washington, D.C.: The Brookings Institution, 1987.

Blair, Bruce. *Strategic Command and Control.* Washington, D.C.: The Brookings Institution, 1985.

Borden, William Liscum. *There Will Be No Time.* New York: Macmillan, 1946.

Bryan, Robert, and Lawrence H. Larsen. *The Eisenhower Administration 1953–1961: A Documentary History.* New York: Random House, 1974.

Bunn, George. *Arms Control by Committee; Managing Negotiations with the Russians.* Stanford, CA: Stanford University Press, 1992.

Carter, Ashton B., William J. Perry, and John D. Steinbruner. *A New Concept of Cooperative Security.* Washington, D.C.: The Brookings Institution, 1992.

Cohen, Avner. *Israel and the Bomb.* New York: Columbia University Press, 1998.

Cupitt, Richard T. *Reluctant Champions: U.S. Presidential Policy and Strategic Export Controls.* New York: Routledge Press, 2000.

Davis, Zachary, et al. *Proliferation Control Regimes: Background and Status.* Washington, D.C.: U.S. Congressional Research Service, 1995.

Davis, Zachary, and Benjamin Frankel, eds. *The Proliferation Puzzle: Why Nuclear Weapons Spread and What Results.* London: Frank Cass, 1993.

Downs, Charles. *Over the Line: North Korea's Negotiating Strategy.* Washington, D.C.: AEI Press, 1999.

Eisenhower, Dwight D. *Mandate for Change.* Garden City, NY: Doubleday & Company, 1963.

Findlay, Trevor, ed. *Chemical Weapons and Missile Proliferation.* Boulder, CO: Lynne Rienner Publishers, 1991.

Fukuyama, Francis. *The End of History and the Last Man.* New York: The Free Press, 1992.

Herken, Gregg. *The Winning Weapon.* New York: Vintage Books, 1982.

Kagan, Donald. *On the Origins of War and the Preservation of Peace.* New York: Anchor Books Doubleday, 1996.

Kaplan, Fred. *The Wizards of Armageddon.* New York: Simon and Schuster, 1983.

Lovins, Amory. *Soft Energy Paths: Toward a Durable Peace.* New York: Harper & Row, 1979.

Lyon, Peter. *Eisenhower, Portrait of the Hero.* Boston: Little, Brown and Company, 1974.

Masters, Dexter, and Katherine Way. *One World or None.* New York: McGraw-Hill, 1946.

Nieburg, Harold. *Nuclear Secrecy and Foreign Policy.* Washington, D.C.: Public Affairs Press, 1964.

Nolan, Janne. *Guardians of the Arsenal: The Politics of Nuclear Strategy.* New York: New Republic Book, Basic Books, 1989.

Noland, Marcus. *Avoiding the Apocalypse: The Future of the Two Koreas.* Washington, D.C.: Institute for International Economics, 2000.

Oberdorfer, Don. *The Two Koreas: A Contemporary History.* Reading, MA: Addison-Wesley, 1997.

Perkovich, George. *India's Nuclear Bomb.* Berkeley, CA: University of California Press, 1999.

Pilat, Joseph, ed. *Atoms for Peace: An Analysis after Thirty Years.* Boulder, CO: Westview Press, 1985.

Quester, George. *Nuclear Diplomacy.* New York: Dunellen Company, 1970.

Rhinelander, John B., and Adam M. Scheinman. *At the Nuclear Crossroads.* Lanham, MD: University Press of America, 1995.

Rhodes, Richard. *Dark Sun: The Making of the Hydrogen Bomb.* New York: Simon and Schuster, 1995.

Sagan, Scott D. *The Limits of Safety: Organizations, Accidents, and Nuclear Weapons.* Princeton, NJ: Princeton University Press, 1993.

Sagan, Scott D., and Kenneth N. Waltz. *The Spread of Nuclear Weapons.* New York: W. W. Norton, 1995.

Scheinman, Lawrence: *Atomic Energy Policy in France under the Fourth Republic.* Princeton, NJ: Princeton University Press, 1965.

———.*The International Atomic Energy Agency and World Nuclear Order.* Washington, D.C.: Resources for the Future, 1987.

Seldon, Robert W. *Reactor Plutonium and Nuclear Explosives.* Livermore, CA: Lawrence Livermore Laboratory, 1978.

Singer, Max, and Aaron Wildavsky. *The Real World Order: Zones of Peace, Zones of Turmoil.* Chatham, NJ: Chatham House Publishers, 1993.

Smith, Alice Kimball. *A Peril and a Hope: The Scientists' Movement in America, 1945–47.* Chicago: University of Chicago Press, 1965.

Smith, Bruce. *The RAND Corporation.* Cambridge: Harvard University Press, 1966.

Sokolski, Henry, ed. *Fighting Proliferation: New Concerns for the 1990s.* Maxwell Air Force Base, AL: Air University Press, 1996.

———. *21st Century Weapons Proliferation: Are We Ready?* London: Frank Cass Publishers, 2001.

Spector, Leonard S. *Nuclear Proliferation Today.* New York: Vintage Books, 1984.

Strauss, Lewis. *Men and Decisions.* Garden City, NY: Doubleday, 1962.

Wohlstetter, Albert, et al. *Swords from Plowshares: The Military Potential of Civilian Nuclear Energy.* Chicago: University of Chicago Press, 1979.

MONOGRAPHS AND REPORTS

Ad Hoc Working Group on Non-Proliferation and Arms Control. *Non-Proliferation and Arms Control: Issues and Options for the Clinton Administration.* Washington, D.C.: Ad Hoc Working Group on Non-Proliferation and Arms Control, January 1993.

Albright, David. *Separated Civil Plutonium Inventories: Current and Future Directions.* Washington, D.C.: Institute for Science and International Security Press, 2000.

Albright, David, and Lauren Barbour. *Plutonium Watch: Separated Plutonium Inventories Continue to Grow.* Washington, D.C.: Institute for Science and International Security Press, 1999.

American Academy of Arts and Sciences. *The Nth Country Problem: A World-Wide Survey of Nuclear Weapons Capabilities.* Washington, D.C.: National Planning Association, 1959.

Blank, Stephen. *The Dynamics of Russian Arms Sales to China.* Carlisle Barracks, PA: Strategic Studies Institute, U.S. Army War College, 1997.

Carnegie Endowment for International Peace. *The Counter-Proliferation Debate.* Washington, D.C.: Carnegie Endowment for International Peace, November 17, 1993.

Center for Counterproliferation Research. *The Impact of the Proliferation of Nuclear, Biological, and Chemical Weapons on the United States Navy.* Washington, D.C.: Center for Counterproliferation Research, National Defense University, 1996.

———. *U.S. Nuclear Policy in the 21st Century.* Washington, D.C.: Center for Counterproliferation Research, National Defense University, 1998.

Chow, Brian G., and Kenneth A. Solomon. *Limiting the Spread of Weapon-Usable Fissile Materials*. Santa Monica, CA: RAND, MDA903–90-C-0004; October 1993.

Chow, Brian G., et al. *A Concept for Strategic Materials Accelerated Removal Talks (SMART)*. Santa Monica, CA: RAND DRU-1338-DoE, April 1996.

Chow, Brian G., Richard H. Speier, and Gregory S. Jones. *The Proposed Fissile-Material Production Cutoff: Next Steps*. Santa Monica, CA: RAND, MR-586-OSD, 1995.

Davidson, William C., Marvin I. Kalkstein, and Christophe Hohenemser. *The Nth Country Problem and Arms Control*. Washington, D.C.: National Planning Association, 1960.

Gilinsky, Victor. *Nuclear Blackmail: The 1994 U.S.-Democratic People's Republic of Korea Agreed Framework on North Korea's Nuclear Program*. Stanford, CA: Hoover Institution, 1997.

Goldman, Frank Gibson. *The International Legal Ramifications of United States Counter-Proliferation Strategy*. Newport, RI: Center for Naval Warfare Studies, April 1997.

Goldman, Stuart, Kenneth Katzman, Robert D. Shuey, and Carl E. Behrens. "Russian Missile Technology and Nuclear Reactor Transfers to Iran." *CRS Long Report for Congress 98–299*, Washington, D.C.: Congressional Research Service, 1998.

Greenberg, Eldon V. C. *The NPT and Plutonium: Application of NPT Prohibitions to "Civilian" Nuclear Equipment, Technology and Materials Associated with Reprocessing and Plutonium Use*. Washington, D.C.: Nuclear Control Institute, 1993.

Joeck, Neil. *Maintaining Nuclear Stability in South Asia*. Adelphi Paper 312. Oxford: Oxford University Press for the IISS, 1997.

Leites, Nathan. *Once More about What We Should Not Do Even in the Worst Case: The Assured Destruction Attack*. Santa Monica, CA: California Arms Control and Foreign Policy Seminar, 1974.

Leventhal, Paul. "IAEA's Safeguards Shortcomings—A Critique." Washington, DC: Nuclear Control Institute, September 12, 1994.

Millhollin, Gary. Wisconsin Project on Nuclear Arms Control. *U.S. Exports to China 1988–1998: Fueling Proliferation*. Washington, D.C.: Wisconsin Project on Nuclear Arms Control, April 1999.

National Association of Manufacturers. *Export Control Reform: A Key to U.S. Export Success: Policy Recommendations*. Washington, D.C.: National Association of Manufacturers, June 1993.

National Planning Association. *1970 Without Arms Control*. Washington, D.C.: National Planning Association, May 1958.

O'Brien, Matthew. "C3I Upgrades for Developing Nations' Missile Operations." Alexandria, VA: Institute for Defense Analyses, 1992.

Panel on the Future Design and Implementation of U.S. National Security Export Controls. *Finding Common Ground: U.S. Export Controls in a Changed Global Environment*. Washington, D.C.: National Academy Press, 1991.

Pikayev, Alexander A., Leonard S. Spector, Elina V. Kirichenko, and Ryan Gibson. *Russia, the US and the Missile Technology Control Regime*. Adelphi Paper 317. London: Institute for International Security Studies, 1998.

Rauf, Tariq, Mary Beth Nikitin, and Jenni Rissanen. *Inventory of International Non-proliferation Organizations and Regimes*. Monterey, CA: Center for Nonproliferation Studies, 2000.

Rowen, Henry S. *Catch-Up: Why Poor Countries Are Becoming Richer, Democratic, Increasingly Peaceable, and Sometimes More Dangerous*. Stanford, CA: Asia/Pacific Research Center, August 1999.

Schearzbach, David A. *Iran's Nuclear Program: Energy or Weapons?* Washington, D.C.: Natural Resources Defense Council, 1995.

Speier, Richard *"The Missile Technology Control Regime: Case Study of a Multilateral Negotiation."* Washington, D.C.: United States Institute of Peace, SG-31–95, 1995. (Available from USIP upon request)

Timberbaev, Roland M. "A Major Milestone in Controlling Nuclear Exports." Monterey, CA: Center for Russian and Eurasian Studies, Monterey Institute of International Studies, 1992.

Viner, Jacob. *International Economics: Studies by Jacob Viner*. Glencoe, IL: The Free Press, 1951.

Wohlstetter, A. J., F. S. Hoffman, R. J. Lutz, and H. S. Rowen. *Selection and Use of Strategic Air Bases*. Santa Monica, CA: The RAND Corporation, R-266, April 1954.

Wohlstetter, Albert, et al. *Towards a New Consensus on Nuclear Technology*. vol. II (Supporting Papers, Arms Control and Disarmament Agency Report No. PH-78-04-832-33).

Wooley, Steve. "Proliferation of Precision Navigation Technologies and Security Implications for the U.S." Alexandria, VA: Institute for Defense Analyses, December 9, 1991.

ARTICLES

Arkin, William M., and Robert S. Norris. "U.S. Nuclear Forces, 2000." *Bulletin of the Atomic Scientists* (May/June 2000): 70.

———. "Global Nuclear Stockpiles, 1945–2000." *Bulletin of the Atomic Scientists* (March/April 2000): 79.

———. "Russian Strategic Nuclear Forces." *Bulletin of the Atomic Scientists* (March/April 1998): 70–71

———. "World Plutonium Inventories." *Bulletin of the Atomic Scientists* (September/October 1999): 71.

Backus, P. H. "Finite Deterrence, Controlled Retaliation." *United States Naval Institute Proceedings* (March 1959): 23–29.

Barletta, Michael. "Chemical Weapons in the Sudan: Allegations and Evidence." *The Nonproliferation Review* 6, no.1 (1998): 115–36.

Bechhoefer, Bernard B. "Negotiating the IAEA." In Bernard B. Bechhoefer, ed. *Postwar Negotiations for Arms Control*. Washington, D.C.: The Brookings Institution, 1961, 156–165.

Blackwill, Robert D., and Ashton B. Carter. "The Role of Intelligence." In Robert Blackwill and Albert Carnesale, eds., *New Nuclear Nations: Consequences for U.S. Policy*. New York: Council on Foreign Relations Press, 1993.

Bowen, Clayton, and Daniel Woulven. "Command and Control Challenges in South Asia." *The Nonproliferation Review* (Spring/Summer 1999): 25–35.

Byman, Daniel. "A Farewell to Arms Inspections." *Foreign Affairs* (January/February 2000): 119–132.

Carter, Ashton B., and Celeste Johnson. "Beyond the Counterproliferation Initiative to a Revolution in Counterproliferation Affairs." *National Security Studies Quarterly* (Summer 1999): 83–90.

Chafetz, Glenn. "The End of the Cold War and the Future of Nuclear Nonproliferation: An Alternative to the Neo-Realist Perspective," *Security Studies* 2 (Spring/Summer 1993): 128–146.

Cohen, Avner. "Stumbling into Opacity: The United States, Israel, and the Atom, 1960–63." *Security Studies* 4, no. 2 (Winter 1994): 199–200.

Cohen, Eliot A. "A Revolution in Warfare." *Foreign Affairs* 75, no. 2 (March/April 1996): 37–54.

Eisenstein, Maurice. "Third World Missiles and Nuclear Proliferation." *The Washington Quarterly* (Summer 1982): 112–115.

Fetter, Steve. "A Comprehensive Transparency Regime for Warheads and Fissile Materials. *Arms Control Today* (January/February 1999): 4.

FitzSimonds, James. "Intelligence and the Revolution in Military Affairs." In Roy Godson, Ernest R. May, and Gary Schmitt, eds. *US Intelligence at the Crossroads: Agenda for Reform*. Washington, D.C.: Brassey's, 1995.

Freedman, Lawrence. "The Strategy of Hiroshima." *The Journal of Strategic Studies* (May 1978): 76–97.

Gallois, Pierre M. "Nuclear Aggression and National Suicide." *The Reporter*, November 18, 1958, 22–26.

Garrity, Patrick J. "Implications of the Persian Gulf War for Regional Powers." *The Washington Quarterly* (Summer 1993): 153–170.

Gilinsky, Victor. "Plutonium from U.S.-Supplied LWRs for North Korea: Do We Have to Worry About It?" Presented before the Forum on Prompting International Scientific, Technological and Economic Cooperation in the Korean Peninsula: Enhancing Stability and International Dialogue, Instituto Diplomatico, Rome, Italy, June 1–2, 2000, published at: http://www.wizard.net/~npec.

———. "Restraining the Spread of Nuclear Weapons: A Walk on the Supply Side." In Jed C. Snyder and Samuel F. Wells, Jr., eds. *Limiting Nuclear Proliferation*. Cambridge, MA: Ballinger Publishing Company, 1985.

Goldfischer, David. "Rethinking the Unthinkable after the Cold War: Toward Long-Term Nuclear Policy Planning." *Security Studies* 7, no. 4 (Summer 1998): 165–94.

Goldschmidt, Bertrand. "The Origins of the International Atomic Energy Agency." *International Atomic Energy Agency Bulletin* (August 1977): 18–19.

Heisbourg, François. "The Prospects for Nuclear Stability Between India and Pakistan." *Survival* (Winter 1998–99): 77–92.

Inglis, David. "The Fourth Country Problem: Let's Stop at Three." *Bulletin of the Atomic Scientists* (January 1959): 22–26.

Kay, David. "Detection and Denial: Iraq and Beyond." *The Washington Quarterly* 18, no. 1 (Winter 1995): 85–105.

Krepinevich, Andrew F. "Cavalry to Computer: The Pattern of Military Revolutions." *The National Interest* (Fall 1994): 30–42.

Lake, Anthony. "A Year of Decisions: Arms Control and Nonproliferation in 1995." *The Nonproliferation Review*, (Winter 1995): 55–59.

Lavoy, Peter R. "Nuclear Myths and the Causes of Nuclear Proliferation." *Security Studies* (Spring/Summer 1993).

Mahnken, Thomas G. "America's Next War." *The Washington Quarterly* (Summer 1993): 171–84.

———. "A Critical Appraisal of the Defense Counterproliferation Initiative." *National Security Studies Quarterly* (Summer 1999): 91–102.

Milhollin, Gary. "India's Missiles—With a Little Help from Our Friends."*Bulletin of the Atomic Scientists* (May 1989): 31–36.

Muller, Harold, and Mitchell Reiss. "Counterproliferation: Putting New Wine in Old Bottles." *The Washington Quarterly* (Spring 1995): 143–54.

Ogilvie-White, Tanya. "Is there a Theory of Nuclear Proliferation? An Analysis of the Contemporary Debate." *The Nonproliferation Review* (Fall 1996): 43–60.

Oppenheimer, J. Robert. "Atomic Weapons and American Policy." *Foreign Affairs* 31, no. 4 (Spring 1953): 525–35.

Orlov, Vladimir, and William C. Potter. "The Mystery of the Sunken Gyros." *Bulletin of the Atomic Scientists* (November–December 1998), 34–39.

Pipes, Daniel. "Muslim Exceptionalism: Why the End of History Won't Be Easy." In Henry Sokolski, ed. *21st Century Weapons Proliferation: Are We Ready?* London: Frank Cass, 2001.

Rathjens, George W., Jr. "Deterrence and Defense." *Bulletin of the Atomic Scientists* (September 1958): 225–28.

"Report to the Secretary of War—June, 1945." *Bulletin of the Atomic Scientists* (May 1, 1946): 2–4.

Ridenour, Louis N. "There is No Defense." In Dexter Masters and Katherine Way, eds. *One World or None*, New York: McGraw-Hill, 1946, 33–38.

Rosenberg, David Alan. "The Origins of Overkill: Nuclear Weapons and American Strategy, 1945–1960." *International Security* 7, no.4 (Spring 1983): 3–71.

———. "A Smoking, Radiation Ruin at the End of Two Hours." *International Security* (Winter 1981–1982): 3–17.

Rowen, Henry. "Why a Rich, Democratic and (Perhaps) Peaceful Era is Ahead," In Henry Sokolski, ed. *21st Century Weapons Proliferation: Are We Ready?* London: Frank Cass, 2001, 108, 112.

Rydell, Randy J. "Giving Nonproliferation Norms Teeth: Sanctions and the NPPA." *The Nonproliferation Review* (Winter 1999): 1–19.

Schaffer, Ronald. "American Military Ethics in World War II: The Bombing of German Civilians." *The Journal of American History* (September 1980): 318–34.

Schmidt, Fritz W. "The Zangger Committee: Its History and Future Role." *The Nonproliferation Review* (Fall 1994): 38–44.

Schneider, Barry R. "Counterforce." In Peter Hayes, ed. *Countering the Proliferation and Use of Weapons of Mass Destruction*. New York: McGraw-Hill, 1998.

Simons, Howard. "World-Wide Capabilities for Production and Control of Nuclear Weapons." *Daedalus* 88, no. 3 (Summer 1959): 385–409.

Soapes, Thomas F. "A Cold Warrior Seeks Peace: Eisenhower's Strategy for Nuclear Disarmament." *Diplomatic History* (Winter 1979–1980): 15.

Sokolski, Henry. "Curbing Proliferation's Legitimization." *Nonproliferation Review* (Winter 1995): 1–4.

———. "Fighting Proliferation with Intelligence." In Henry Sokolski, ed. *Fighting Proliferation: New Concerns for the 1990s*. Maxwell Air Force Base, AL: Air University Press, 1996, 277–98.

———. "Nonapocalyptic Proliferation: A New Strategic Threat?" *The Washington Quarterly* (Spring 1994): 115–27.

Spector, Leonard S. "Neo-Nonproliferation." *Survival* (Spring 1995): 66–85.

Speier, Richard. "The Missile Technology Control Regime." In Trevor Findlay, ed. *Chemical Weapons and Missile Proliferation*. Boulder, CO: Lynne Rienner Publishers, 1991.

———. "An NPT for Missiles?" In Henry Sokolski, ed. *Fighting Proliferation: New Concerns for the 1990s*. Maxwell Air Force Base, AL: Air University Press, 1996, 57–74.

Talbott, Strobe. "Democracy and the National Interest." *Foreign Affairs* (November/December 1996): 47–63.

Timmerman, Kenneth. "Fighting Proliferation Through Democracy: A Competitive Strategies Approach toward Iran." In Henry Sokolski, ed. *Prevailing in a Well-Armed World*. Carlisle, PA: Strategic Studies Institute, 2000, 111–32.

Weiss, Leonard. "The Concept of 'Timely Warning' in the Nuclear Nonproliferation Act of 1978." Minority Staff Position Paper, Senate Subcommittee on Energy, Nuclear Proliferation and Governmental Processes, April 1, 1985.

Williams, Chris. "DoD's Counterproliferation Initiative; A Critical Assessment." In Henry Sokolski, ed. *Fighting Proliferation: New Concerns for the 1990s*, Maxwell Air Force Base, AL: Air University Press, 1996, 249–56.

Wohlstetter, Albert. "The Delicate Balance of Terror." *Foreign Affairs* (January 1959): 211–34.

———. "The Military Potential of Civilian Nuclear Energy." *Minerva* (Autumn-Winter 1977): 387–538.

———. "NATO and the N+1 Country." *Foreign Affairs* (April 1961): 355–87.

Wohlstetter, Albert, et al. "The Spread of Nuclear Bombs: Predictions, Premises, Policies." Vol. I-1 of *Can We Make Nuclear Power Compatible with Limiting the Spread of Nuclear Weapons?* Los Angeles: Pan Heuristics, November 15, 1976, ERDA Contract E (49–1)-3747, 9–32, 89–108.

Index

About the Author

HENRY D. SOKOLSKI is Executive Director of the Nonproliferation Policy Education Center. From 1989 to early 1993 Mr. Sokolski served as Deputy for Nonproliferation Policy in the Office of Secretary of Defense Richard Cheney. In addition to his government service, Mr. Sokolski has lectured and written extensively on proliferation issues.